# Called to Be a People of the Gospel

# Called to Be a People of the Gospel

St. Paul's New Testament Letter to the Ephesians

Earl F. Palmer

FOREWORD BY
M. Craig Barnes

CASCADE *Books* • Eugene, Oregon

CALLED TO BE A PEOPLE OF THE GOSPEL
St. Paul's New Testament Letter to the Ephesians

Copyright © 2022 Earl F. Palmer. All rights reserved. Except for brief quotations in critical publications or reviews, no part of this book may be reproduced in any manner without prior written permission from the publisher. Write: Permissions, Wipf and Stock Publishers, 199 W. 8th Ave., Suite 3, Eugene, OR 97401.

Cascade Books
An Imprint of Wipf and Stock Publishers
199 W. 8th Ave., Suite 3
Eugene, OR 97401

www.wipfandstock.com

PAPERBACK ISBN: 978-1-6667-3112-5
HARDCOVER ISBN: 978-1-6667-2415-8
EBOOK ISBN: 978-1-6667-2454-7

## *Cataloguing-in-Publication data:*

Names: Palmer, Earl F., author. | Barnes, M. Craig, foreword.

Title: Called to be a people of the gospel : St. Paul's New Testament letter to the Ephesians / by Earl F. Palmer ; foreword by M. Craig Barnes.

Description: Eugene, OR: Cascade Books, 2022 | Includes bibliographical references.

Identifiers: ISBN 978-1-6667-3112-5 (paperback) | ISBN 978-1-6667-2415-8 (hardcover) | ISBN 978-1-6667-2454-7 (ebook)

Subjects: LCSH: Bible. Ephesians—Commentaries.

Classification: BS2695.53 P40 2022 (print) | BS2695 (ebook)

02/21/23

All scripture quotations are from New Revised Version of the Bible (NSRV) unless otherwise noted.

The photo on the cover shows the ancient arena at the entrance of the city of Ephesus during the life of Paul and it is still in existence.

This book is dedicated to Shirley Green Palmer, my beloved wife and life companion who traveled alongside from a handwritten text on pages of yellow legal pad to printed pages. She has helped me the most and encouraged me, and not only in this book.

# Contents

*Foreword by M. Craig Barnes* | ix

*Preface* | xiii

*Acknowledgments* | xv

Section I: The Journey of a Man from Tarsus (Summary of Paul's Life) | Paul and the Mark of Grace | 1

    Part 1: A Life-Changing Discovery | 3

    Part 2: Travels Throughout the Mediterranean World | 13

    Part 3: Support and Encouragement | 19

Section II: Paul Reaches Out to the People of the Gospel (Exposition of Text) | The Message that Paul Sends Unfolds as a Prayer | 25

    Part 4: Belovedness Revealed (Ephesians 1) | 27

    Part 5: Disruption Occurs (Ephesians 2) | 34

    Part 6: Grace Intervenes (Ephesians 3) | 50

Section III: Paul Offers Advice for the People of the Gospel (Exposition of Text) | The Appeal to Lead a Life Worthy | 59

    Part 7: The Truth of the Gospel Is the Axiom (Ephesians 4) | 62

    Part 8: Walk in the Light (Ephesians 5) | 91

    Part 9: Stand with Strength (Ephesians 6) | 105

Postscript | 123

*Appendix I: Resource for Expositional Preaching and Teaching* | 127

*Appendix II: Reflections on the Life of Paul* | 138

*Appendix III: Reflections on the Letter to the Ephesians* | 140

*Appendix IV: Strategies to Follow in Small Group Bible Studies* | 149

*References that Aided in the Study of Ephesians* | 153

# Foreword

THE REVEREND EARL PALMER has been a faithful expositor of the Bible for over sixty-five years since he graduated from Princeton Theological Seminary. But his love for Scripture can be traced back to his years as a college student at UC Berkeley, where he began to attend a student-led Bible study. As he states in this book, "It was there that my discovery of Jesus Christ of the Bible made all of the difference. A new wholeness began to take shape in me."

He is always quick to acknowledge the early influencers in his life like Dr. Robert Boyd Munger, Miss Henrietta Mears, and Dr. John A. Mackay, who was the president of our seminary. And anyone who has heard his teaching or read his books know how much he has been shaped by the writings of C. S. Lewis, Fyodor Dostoevsky, and Karl Barth, all of whom he quotes often, including in this commentary.

But it was the biblical text that led him to Jesus Christ, and it has always been his primary teacher. This is the root of his lifelong commitment to expositional teaching and preaching, by which he means allowing the text to make its own point about the gospel that brings us to Jesus Christ, so that the listener is drawn into the words of the Bible in such a way as to say, "Oh, I see the truth of this for myself and for our world."

I have heard Rev. Palmer teach at many conferences and retreats, and preach at the churches he has served over his long ministry as a pastor. He always arrives at the podium or pulpit with his worn Bible and a yellow legal tab filled with notes. Every presentation or sermon is so engaging not only because of its content, but also because he's just so excited about what he is going to say. One gets the feeling that he has spent the week mining the text carefully, and has discovered another precious gem that he can't wait to show the congregation. As he lifts one gem of truth and penetrating insight from the text after another, those of us in the pews are invited into the same experience he had years ago in his college Bible study. And we too discover more of Jesus Christ and the "new wholeness" he is offering to us, the church, and our society that is in dire need of his salvation.

This commentary on Paul's Epistle to the Ephesians offers a classic glimpse into Earl Palmer's understanding of expositional teaching. He begins by taking the time to present the context of the ancient culture of Ephesus as well as the life of the apostle who wrote the letter. Later in the book he draws out illuminating insights from this background. With each passage he engages in careful exegesis of the verses, demonstrating his proficiency with Koine Greek, all in the belief that if you understood the text as the first readers did, it would make its own claims upon your life. He also places this letter in the larger context of Paul's writings, especially Romans, in order to draw together theological affirmations about the work of God among us.

As a pastor, Rev. Palmer takes delight in showing his reader how the Bible's own understanding of its theological terms reveal the hope, joy, love, and peace of lives that are restored in Christ.

For example, in these pages he explains grace not just as a means of finding forgiveness, but also as "being surprised by the love of God." He roots this in Paul's own surprising discovery of grace on the road to Damascus, which is why Paul fills his letter to the Ephesians with repeated calls to see the transformation that is available to us by this same grace he encountered.

As the apostle Paul claims, and Rev. Palmer echoes, this surprising grace lifts up our lives from the dark places they had fallen:

> But God, who is rich in mercy, out of the great love with which he loved us, even when we were dead through our trespasses, made us alive together with Christ—by grace you have been saved—and raised up with him in the heavenly places in Christ Jesus . . . (2:4–6)

## FOREWORD

This passage that begins with "But God" immediately follows Paul's description of how much damage we have done to ourselves and to others through our sin. "You were dead through the trespasses and sins in which you once lived . . . and were by nature children of wrath, like everyone else," Paul wrote (2:1–3). "But God" saves us by grace, makes us alive, and raises us up out of the tombs into which we had settled in this life. "But God" gives us life together with Christ. "But God" is the turning point of the gospel.

In Earl Palmer's words, "Here we encounter the answer of the gospel to the universal longing for human identity, as we seek to know who we are. We are reminded that our basic identity as human beings is rooted in God's love for us. . . . The sheer grace of this belovedness is the primary marker of our identity."

As this commentary claims, this now makes us safe to others, and safe to ourselves. Now, as it says, "we are made ready to *do* good deeds. We are created and given by Christ the kindness of his love, so that we may share that grace with others as a new way of life."

Then following the apostle's development of thought, Rev. Palmer demonstrates that it is only the grace of God that calls the diverse church together, holds it together, and equips it for the mission of offering grace to a world that knows so little of it.

Grace is just one of the profound theological and spiritual themes that rise out of the exposition found here. Rev. Palmer also draws our attention to what the Letter to the Ephesians has to show us about the church and its mission, provides counsel for living the Christian life, and offers pastoral insights about what it means to be centered in Christ. Along the way he keeps showing us what these insights meant to Paul, to the Church at Ephesus, and what it all can mean for readers who are called to live as a people of the gospel.

Finally, it is important to note that this commentary was written as the author approached his ninetieth birthday. What it offers the reader is an opportunity to sit at the feet of a faithful Bible expositor who is offering not only insights, but also his lifelong devotion to the holy text that can keep surprising us with the gracious love of God.

M. Craig Barnes
Princeton Theological Seminary

# Preface

FOR ME IT HAS been a personal privilege and challenge to study St. Paul's New Testament Letter to the Ephesians. I see two of Paul's letters in the New Testament as clarifying what I believe and what I do as a Christian. First is the Letter to the Romans, which was written in the middle of Paul's ministry. In it, he presents a deep understanding of the source of the gospel—the righteous character of God that has broken through to bring truth and grace to the world. The second is the Letter to the Ephesians, where Paul writes about the people of the gospel. Here, he offers guidance for us on how to live as followers of Jesus. I am drawn to his words by my own timely need to listen to Paul as he writes from prison in Rome at the midpoint of his century. This book is important to me.

As background, it is of interest to realize that Paul had always wanted to go to Rome. He had traveled for years throughout the Mediterranean world to teach the gospel. When he finally arrived in Rome, it was not as a world leader, a statesman, but as a prisoner. While in captivity he continued to write letters to the people and places of his years of teaching ministry, where he made friends and planted churches.

From the prison that held him for over two years, he wrote to the people he loved and to a city he loved, Ephesus, where he had taught for two and a half years. I view the Letter to the Ephesians as a companion letter to the Letter to the Romans. Paul wants the people to understand the message of Jesus and to view a fellowship that is worldwide, with members from every tribe and every place.

Ephesians is an encouraging book that seemed just right for the first century, and it is just right for the twenty-first century.

PREFACE

Paul's vision is broad and generous, totally committed both to the truth of the good news of Jesus Christ and to the grace of the Lord that serves to bring equilibrium into our lives. For this reason, I have titled the book *Called to Be a People of the Gospel: St. Paul's New Testament Letter to the Ephesians*. In this expositional commentary, I hope to underscore the mandate Paul suggests for how to live as followers of Jesus and to make what he faced in his time come alive.

Join me in this study of a letter that will open your heart and mind to the message Paul has for us today. I guarantee you will break into song when you read chapter 3.

Earl F. Palmer

# Acknowledgments

To begin, I first want to say thank you to my team, the board of Earl Palmer Ministries. These brothers and sisters have inspired me and given me the incentive to write this commentary. Their names include Alex Berezow, Dick Greiling, Scott Hardman, Paul Lange, George Nethercutt, Melissa Reis, Mary Snyder, Gordon Stephenson, and Tony Whatley, chairman.

Over the past years, twelve young men have served as study assistants. They met the challenge of reading my handwriting, reminded me of emails to be answered, made arrangements for in-person events, made sure that I got to meetings on time when crossing time zones, added their ideas and creativity to not only events but also the printed newsletters, watched out for me and sat in airports en route, drove me across miles to speak at church gatherings, sat in my kitchen discussing the activities on hand and drank coffee when I later discovered they preferred tea or water, made sense of the website (a new world for me), cared for people who called out for help when distressed, and shared their experiences as Christians in the ongoing ministries of their own. Thanks to each for the contribution of their talents to Earl Palmer Ministries: Kurt Heineman 2008–2009, Daniel Triller 2009–2010, Roderick Gellner 2010–2011, John Sittser 2011–2012, Dexter Kearney 2012–2013, Chris Thurton 2013–2014, Gray Segars 2014–2015, Stephen Michael 2015–2016, Landon Bennett 2016–2017, Zach Pankratz 2017–2018, Tate Busby 2018–2020, and Jun Kwak 2020–2021.

Words of gratitude go to my forgiving and totally helpful editor, Kathy Gillin, who added her understanding of the gospel to the skill of grammar and organizational format to hold the manuscript together.

In writing this commentary, I have had in mind two groups of people who have inspired me greatly in ministry and in life. Therefore:

I want to express my appreciation for the Earl Palmer Ministries Word and Worship team, Sue Nixon, Walt Wagner, Brian Coon, Dale Roth, Heather Whitney, Tomo Morita, musicians; and to Kay Broweleit, pastor of prayer. And to Bill Levy who handles the recording. I want to especially mention Bruce Hosford, our generous and gracious sponsor.

These are the people who have shown me what a working fellowship of brothers and sisters looks like, how a team works, and why such a group makes all the difference in our journey through life. These are the people who have created a time of inspiration and encouragement for me and those who listen: Word and Worship at Henry Chapel—"An evening hour set apart for worship and personal reflection through music, prayer, and exposition of texts from the Bible." These are the people who have volunteered their time and talents to be there and share with me the good news for a world waiting to hear.

I also want to extend my gratitude to my family, and I especially honor the Mt. Shasta Adventure Team, who during the pandemic traveled by car 500 miles in somewhat tandem style from Seattle, Washington to Mt. Shasta, California and included me in their climbing adventure on the mountain that I have known well in years past, having summited it more than fifty times in my earlier years. And now these were the people who demonstrated what it means to climb step-by-step alongside each other when facing the demands of a looming mountain. For the generation of our grandchildren new to this adventure, it was a unique time to always remember. As with other times of joy and of challenge over the years, their experience reinforced what it means to be a family and share life together. As in this and with other times along life's journey in years past, we were all in it together.

## ACKNOWLEDGMENTS

The trip took four days that began with a nonstop drive from Seattle to Northern California—then added an overnight in the town below the mountain, and the next night on the mountain—and culminated, after the return from the climb, with another night in the town below the mountain and a nonstop drive back to Seattle the next day.

I was the keeper of Camp 1, settled at the Tree House Motel in Mt. Shasta. My role was to keep the food supplies left behind safe from hungry bears. I studied the mountain and visualized their route from the balcony outside my room. The others were at Camp 2—settled at timberline at 8,000 feet, with sleeping bags laid out on the ground for a short night, so as to be ready at 4 a.m. on Saturday for the day of the climb at high elevation.

To report: The route took two of them to 11,000 feet; three to 12,800 feet; and six to the summit at 14,162 feet. Two stayed behind at timberline to tend and guard Camp 2.

Shirley, my wife, kept the originating base camp intact in the Pacific Northwest and followed the journey by car and by foot with reports provided in the age of texting via phone. The family shared words of the ascent with her as a brutal uphill climb, and I helped to keep her calm in the three hours beyond the expected descent as we waited for the climbers to get off the mountain.

What I heard was that the mountaineers valued what it means to climb together on an adventure and feel the support of one another to reach a goal. We all rejoiced in the realization of what it means to face a challenge of such magnitude. At times, life demands determination and grit to keep going. And it was important to realize that climbing a mountain takes patience—always one step at a time.

These climbers were the members of our family—the adult children and their families (eight grandchildren, ages ten to twenty-three). Each one means so much to Shirley and me for all the reasons of love. To the team—Anne Welsh, Sarah Welsh, Emily Welsh; Jon Palmer, Kara Diane Palmer, Drew Palmer, Tommy Palmer; Liz Jacobsen, Eric Jacobsen, Kate Jacobsen, Peter Jacobsen, Emma Jacobsen, and Abe Jacobsen—I commend the words of Paul: ". . . that Christ may dwell in your hearts through faith, that you, being rooted and grounded in love, may have power to comprehend with all the saints what is the breadth and length and height and depth and to know the love of Christ which surpasses knowledge, that you may be filled with all the fullness of God (Eph 3:17–19). I wish them God's blessing.

# Section I

# The Journey of a Man from Tarsus

*(A Brief Summary of Paul's Life)*

## Paul and the Mark of Grace

IN THESE OPENING PAGES, I want to give you an introduction to Paul, whose name has been given to one of the great cathedrals in the world, St. Paul's Cathedral in London. His name has been revered throughout the ages. He was able to make friends of slaves, aristocrats, and even Roman guards. I think he was able to do this because he had experienced such sheer grace that it was in him, and he had to share it. The experience of knowing he was beloved changed his life, and his life then changed the lives of many people in his time and even today. I have learned so much from Paul. He has become my friend, too.

# Part 1: A Life-Changing Discovery

## A Background of Radical Roots

SAUL, LATER NAMED PAUL, grew up in a prosperous Jewish family in Tarsus, a city made famous by the philosopher and teacher Zeno (340–265 BC), the father of Stoicism. Saul inherited the designation as a Roman citizen through his father, who had previously been awarded Roman citizenship. As a well-educated young man, Saul moved to Jerusalem. There he studied under the Pharisee Gamaliel, grandson of the great teacher Hillel. Saul not only became a devoted member of the Pharisee lay movement, but he also identified himself with the movement's extreme faction. While both Gamaliel and Hillel taught in the moderate Pharisee tradition, Saul chose a pathway of strident opposition against Jewish followers of the new way of the Rabbi Jesus, and he broke away from the moderation of Hillel and Gamaliel with the intent to destroy the rising movement.

Writing years later, Paul discloses the extremist position he took early in his life. This apostle to the gentiles and author of the Letter to the Ephesians reveals his past in a speech recorded in the book of Acts. In it, he describes himself and the hardline Pharisee position he once embraced.

> I am a Jew, born in Tarsus in Cilicia, but brought up in this city at the feet of Gamaliel, educated strictly according to our ancestral law, being zealous for God, just as all of you are today. I persecuted this Way up to the point of death by binding both men and women and putting them in prison as the high priest and the whole council of elders can testify about me. From them I also received

letters to the brothers in Damascus, and I went there in order to bind those who were there and to bring them back to Jerusalem for punishment (Acts 22:3-5).

Notice his language choices: "strictly" . . . "ancestral law" . . . "being zealous for God." This is the language of young men and women who had left behind the taming restraints of Gamaliel or even sensible caution, and who were determined to use aggressive strategies against those who had become enemies of their severe "zeal-for-God" convictions. Actions, even violence, were welcomed by a new radicalism that was determined to protect the honor of God. This extreme position included punishing others who were understood to be a part of this religious faction's conspiracy against truth. Holding this mindset, Saul approved the brutal stoning of a young deacon named Stephen, a leader in the newly formed people of the Way, who were followers of the risen Jesus (Acts 8:1).

## The Interrupted Mission to Damascus

*(This narrative appears with variations in Acts 9:1-22, Acts 22:1-16, and Acts 26:12-23.)*
Fortunately for this angry young man, and for us too, while traveling on the road to Damascus with letters from the high priest to secure the arrest of Jews who had become followers of Jesus, Saul has an encounter. At midday, he is met with a blinding vision. He falls to the ground and hears the words, "Saul, Saul why do you persecute me? It hurts you to kick against the goads" (Acts 26:14). Temporarily blinded, Saul asks, "Who are you, Lord?" The answer is clear. "I am Jesus whom you are persecuting. But get up and enter the city and you will be told what you are to do" (Acts 9:5, 6). In this encounter, Jesus does not relate as a conqueror but as a shepherd who has found a lost young man. Saul hears not judgment but surprisingly pastoral words from the risen and living Jesus Christ. "Saul got up from the ground, and though his eyes were open he could see nothing; so they led him by the hand and brought him into Damascus" (Acts 9:8-9).

## PART 1: A LIFE-CHANGING DISCOVERY

It happens also that the Lord appears in a vision to a disciple named Ananias and tells him to go to the house on the street called Straight and "look for a man of Tarsus named Saul," which he does (Acts 9:10–12). And there in the house of ordinary believers in Damascus, Saul is cared for and his eyesight is restored. In that fellowship, he is baptized as a new believer in the risen Jesus.

Shortly thereafter, Saul returns with their blessing to Jerusalem. However, the believers in Jerusalem are afraid of him. The people in that fellowship—led by Barnabas, a key leader in the church of Jerusalem—encourage Saul to return to his family city, Tarsus. In the midst of these times, he renames himself, as was common in Roman tradition. His new name is "Paul." From Paul's letter to the Galatians, we know that he stays away from Jerusalem for three years (Gal 1:17).

Nothing would be the same again for this once-angry young extremist, who had so strongly adhered to the strict rendering of the Law. Paul had met the living Jesus Christ. And he was tenderly cared for by a small company of first-century believers in Damascus, where he regained his strength. From this time forward, Paul would never forget his two-part transforming encounter.

He would always be a man who had experienced the love of Jesus Christ, who was able to find a man like Saul and welcome him with grace. The encounter made all the difference to his self-understanding, and also to his growing intellectual understanding of what had happened to him on that afternoon. Many years later, a great theologian of the twentieth century, Karl Barth, would describe what is meant by the term, "the centered faith in Christ." In his commentary *Dogmatics in Outline*, Barth discusses the Apostles' Creed:

> "Tell me how it stands with your Christology and I shall tell you who you are." This is the point at which ways diverge, and the point at which is fixed the relation between theology and philosophy, and the relation between knowledge of God and knowledge of men, the relation between revelation and reason, the relation between Gospel and Law, the relation between God's truth and man's truth, the relation between outer and

inner, the relation between theology and politics. At this point everything becomes clear or unclear, bright or dark. For here we are standing at the centre. And however high and mysterious and difficult everything we want to know might seem to us, yet we may also say that this is just where everything becomes quite simple, quite straightforward, quite childlike. Right here in this centre, in which as a Professor of Systematic Theology I must call to you, "Look! This is the point now! Either knowledge, or the greatest folly!"—here I am in front of you, like a teacher in Sunday school facing his kiddies who has something to say which a mere four-year-old can really understand. "The world was lost, but Christ was born, rejoice!"[1]

What happened to Paul in Damascus changed him, too. There, he also experienced the fellowship and grace of the followers of Jesus, who restored his health, baptized him, and sent him back to Jerusalem a new man. Luke writes, "For several days he was with the disciples in Damascus and immediately he began to proclaim Jesus in the synagogues, saying 'He is the Son of God.' All who heard him were amazed and said, 'Is not this the man who made havoc in Jerusalem among those who invoked this name?'" (Acts 9:19–21). Paul would always be a man who loved Jesus Christ and a man in fellowship with the church of Jesus Christ.

This body of believers, either small or large, is what we call the gathering, the church. In my own life, I have been struck by these two same discoveries that Paul made: the living Jesus Christ, and the gathered believers.

## My personal journey

I wrote a poem to share these common strands in my journey. It tells of the discovery of that worshiping house that has played such a role in my own life. Whether in Damascus or Berkeley, in Seattle or Washington, DC, or in Manila, I have been nourished and then sent out to teach and share the open door of that house.

1. Barth, *Dogmatics in Outline*, 66–67.

PART 1: A LIFE-CHANGING DISCOVERY

## I Know a House

I know a house that took me in to send me out
And I keep finding this house in all of the
places in my life as if it were as itinerant as I

My first memory of this place I call a house
is of friendly fragrances
the smell of evening suppers and coffee
brewing, sometimes of old wooden doors that
are out of fashion and sometimes the new
aroma of children laughing

I came to know the people of this house
who took me in to send me out
because they taught me here about the
owner of the house and in time I
learned his name

I always loved best of all the main room
right at the center in this house
a room that always seems vast in size to me
with its grand sounds solemn and joyous
and the flood of color on both sunny and cloudy days

I learned the memory of a royal past because of this house
and like a waterfall cataract of some mysterious river
that flowed around its open door
I felt the powerful surprise of hope and resolve

I know this house and wherever I go I find
it either settled in or precariously perched
yet always the house that takes me in
to send me out[2]

---

2. Earl Palmer, unpublished poem, 2005.

SECTION I: THE JOURNEY OF A MAN FROM TARSUS

## The Importance of Antioch

*The role of this city in Paul's life as a changed man/person.*

Antioch played a key role in the spread of the gospel. In the book Acts of the Apostles, author Luke narrates and records the events, places, and people at the beginning of Paul's public ministry, in which he witnessed to the gospel in the Greek world.

> Now those who were scattered because of the persecution that took place over Stephen traveled as far as Phoenicia, Cyprus, and Antioch, and they spoke the word to no one except Jews. But among them were some men of Cyprus and Cyrene who, on coming to Antioch, spoke to the Hellenists also, proclaiming the Lord Jesus. The hand of the Lord was with them, and a great number became believers and turned to the Lord. News of this came to the ears of the church in Jerusalem, and they sent Barnabas to Antioch. When he came and saw the grace of God, he rejoiced, and he exhorted them all to remain faithful to the Lord with steadfast devotion; for he was a good man, full of the Holy Spirit and of faith. And a great many people were brought to the Lord. Then Barnabas went to Tarsus to look for Saul, and when he had found him, he brought him to Antioch. So it was that for an entire year they met with the church and taught a great many people, and it was in Antioch that the disciples were first called "Christians" (Acts 11:19–26).

First-century Antioch, located on the Orantes River, was the third largest city in the Roman Empire (Rome itself was largest, followed by Alexandria and then Antioch). Its population exceeded 500,000. Antioch was prosperous because of its favorable harbor, its access to the silk route to the east, and its dependable source of fresh water. The result was a decadence that pervaded the city, a place where money flowed without either industry or hard work to earn it. Antioch was the least respected city in the whole of

## PART 1: A LIFE-CHANGING DISCOVERY

the Roman Empire. Its red-light district, "The Grove of Daphne," was a scandal. Because of that reputation, Roman soldiers were not allowed to have liberty in Antioch.

It was to this large, cynically reckless, and wealthy city that a number of Jewish Christ-followers came to work and trade. It was there where they shared their faith in the Lord Jesus. Many Greeks in this international city were won to faith. Barnabas saw this when he visited Antioch, as described by the writer of Acts. "When Barnabas saw the grace of God, he rejoiced and he exhorted them to remain faithful to the Lord" (Acts 11:23). While Barnabas might have noticed the marks of decadence in Antioch, he saw, instead, the love of God at work in this unlikely place. He decided to find Paul at Tarsus and invite him to join with him and the growing body of believers, as teachers of the gospel of the Lord Jesus. Together, they taught in Antioch for more than a year.

In the text, Luke adds one more sentence. "It was in Antioch that the disciples were first called 'Christians'" (Acts 11:26). Some New Testament interpreters have wondered if at the beginning of their time in Antioch, the term was used as an informal, even critical description. I like to imagine words such as "It is Christ this and Christ that" and/or "These people are always talking about Christ," so that it might have been used as a mark of ridicule or mockery. But later, as earnest and intelligent folk joined the fellowship, the believers won respect from the population. The description "Christian" at last became an honorable description rather than an insult.

Either way, "Christian" became a truthful explanation of what meant the most to these believers. By then, they had become an international mix of Greeks and Jews, North Africans, Europeans, and Egyptians. St. Paul was a champion of the interracial, intercultural mixture of people who were drawn to Jesus of Nazareth. Jesus's own use of languages opened the opportunity to interact with people across the spectrum of cultures. It may even be that Jesus spoke Greek with an Alexandrian accent, since he probably lived as a small boy, perhaps to age seven or eight, in Alexandria with his mother and father; it was to Alexandria that the holy family fled

## SECTION I: THE JOURNEY OF A MAN FROM TARSUS

from Herod the Great after Jesus's birth. He certainly spoke Galilean Aramaic as an adult, and also the classical Hebrew that a Jewish lad who attended the synagogue would learn.

Two features of the new church believers in Jesus at Antioch should be especially noted. The first is the simplicity in the expression of their faith, as exemplified by the Jewish followers of Jesus from Jerusalem, Cyprus, and Cyrene who came to live in the city. They shared their faith with few words, but those were words of powerful witness. Luke describes this in a short sentence: "... they proclaimed the Lord Jesus ... the hand of the Lord was with them, and a great number became believers and turned to the Lord" (Acts 11:20–21). Perhaps Barnabas encouraged Paul with words such as, "Paul, you can fit into this place." And he did! The other significant fact to recognize is that from the newly formed church fellowship, Paul and Barnabas—together with other traveling companions—were sent out by the church in Antioch to places near and far within the Mediterranean world.

Even though some in Antioch might mock these people and their "Lord Jesus," it has been true down through the centuries that the name of Jesus is always there in front of us. I am reminded of an occasion when as pastor to students at University Presbyterian Church in Seattle, I knew a young man very well. He was in our high school youth group's leadership team. He came one day to inform me that he could not stay with our group or meet with our student leaders or me anymore, because in his heart and mind he no longer could call himself a Christian. This marked his respectful exit from our fellowship, and I thanked him for his honesty, saying I hoped we would see each other again sometime in the future. Soon after that meeting, he left Seattle to go to college. I left Seattle too, with my wife and our two-year-old, and moved to Manila. After six years as pastor at The Union Church of Manila, I was called to become senior pastor at the church where I first became a Christian, First Presbyterian Church of Berkeley, California. I was at that post for twenty-one years, until 1991. One day at a morning service, I recognized my former student, who introduced me to his wife. After the worship service, he shared

## PART 1: A LIFE-CHANGING DISCOVERY

that he and his wife were active Christians together. I will always remember his next words. He said, "You know, Earl, I found that if I dismissed Jesus as an idea, he haunted me as a man, and if I dismissed him as a man, he haunted me as an idea. I really could not get away from him, so I am back and it feels good."

## A Dostoevsky Interlude

*A story from literature gives emphasis.*

No author has captured this enduring power of Jesus of Nazareth as profoundly to me as Fyodor Dostoevsky in his two greatest novels, *Crime and Punishment* and *The Brothers Karamazov*. In the latter work,[3] he makes the point clearly:

Alyósha is the youngest of the Karamazov brothers, about age eighteen, and his middle brother Ivan is about twenty-two. The oldest brother, Dmitry, is accused of murder. Ivan, trained in law, worries about the youngest brother, since Alyósha has become deeply committed and loyal to a godly Russian Orthodox priest, Father Zosima. Ivan invites Alyósha to lunch, hoping to set him free from his devotion to the church, and especially the circle around Zosima. Alyósha is excited to be with Ivan, since Ivan is his hero. But Ivan turns their lunch conversation into a polemic against the historic Russian Orthodox Church and its grim stories of corruption. Alyósha listens without interruption, except for a few respectful questions. Finally, Ivan clearly announces that he won't believe in God and the corrupted church.

Alyósha answers, "Yes, but we have a savior who can forgive our sins because He is without sin and He shed His innocent blood for everyone." Ivan's reply is an unforgettable moment in the story. "I've been wondering why you hadn't brought him up, you Christians always trot out Jesus first." Then Ivan changes the subject. "You know Alyósha, I wrote a kind of poem. I'll let you

3. Dostovesky, *Brothers Karamazov*, 308–32.

hear it, you'll be my first listener," laughs Ivan. "Do you want to hear it?" "I'd like very much to hear it," says Alyósha. Ivan answers, "My tale is called *The Grand Inquisitor*." Then Ivan tells what he calls a tale. *The Grand Inquisitor* has become one of the high-water marks in all of great literature, and it turns out to be a remarkable tribute to Jesus, who sets us free.

The tale features a cardinal, the Grand Inquisitor. He is nearly ninety years old, tall and erect. A prisoner is brought in for trial. The prisoner is Jesus, and he disappoints the inquisitor, who says to Jesus, "you make men free but they want to be happy." The inquisitor waits for the prisoner to answer, but Jesus remains silent. He walks to the old inquisitor and kisses him. "The Kiss sears his heart," and he says, "Go and don't come back any more . . . never . . . never, never."

Then Alyósha surprises Ivan. "Your story is in praise of Jesus, not in disparagement . . . as you claim." At this point, Alyósha stands up and goes over to him without speaking, and kisses him on the lips. "Plagiarism," cries Ivan in a transport of delight. "You stole that from my tale! But thank you all the same."

The tale Ivan tells is done, but the story is not over for Ivan. Like my student leader—like every human being alive—Ivan finds himself mid-story. I believe St. Paul holds this view throughout his ministry with the people in Ephesus: they too find themselves mid-story. This approach conveys grace to many believers and to the many who are still wondering. Paul and Dostoevsky are on the same page.

# Part 2: Travels Throughout the Mediterranean World

## Timothy Joins Paul in Lystra

*Paul travels throughout the Roman Province of Asia on his journey.*

ONE OF THE EARLIEST visits Paul and Barnabas made from Antioch was to the city of Lystra, in the province of Galatia. Luke tells of this exciting visit. Because of the healing of a lame man, a large crowd of local citizens gathered, along with the priest of the local temple of Zeus. In the Lyconian language, they began to praise Barnabas as the god Zeus come down in human form, and Paul as embodying the god Hermes. When Paul and Barnabas realized that the crowd wanted to offer sacrifices, they rushed forward saying, "Friends, why are you doing this? We are mortals just like you . . ." (Acts 14:15). The enraged crowd started to throw stones at Paul. The disciples of Jesus who were in Lystra surrounded Paul and rescued him. A few days later Paul and Barnabas returned to Lystra, and many believers were added to that Christian fellowship. Of special interest to us is that Paul would visit this city in Galatia four times.

On one such occasion, Paul was with Silvanus and Luke, the beloved physician. On this visit, a young man named Timothy joined with Paul for the remaining years of his ministry and writing (Acts 16:1–5). I have often wondered if Timothy might have been one of the Christians who surrounded Paul during that terrifying stoning incident of that first visit. Timothy was to play a major part in all that happened from this time forward, in the narratives written by Luke. From Lystra, Paul and his friends traveled on to Troas and from there into Europe. Later, Paul's earliest New Testament letter would be written to these Christians at Lystra—the book of Galatians.

During the course of his missionary journeys, Paul traveled with his closest team of friends: the beloved physician Luke, who was a Greek, and two younger men—Silas, a Jewish believer, and Timothy, son of a Jewish mother and a Greek father. These four were often joined by others. Together they traveled from Troas into Europe by way of Philippi, which became the first church in Europe and subsequently the entry to the continent. The church at Philippi would later receive a prison letter from Paul.

## Paul's Journey Continues with His Friends on to Ephesus

*He establishes churches as he travels.*

The team then went on to Thessalonica, the capital of Macedonia, where another church was added, to which Paul would later write two letters. The team continued on to Athens. There, Paul stood on Mars Hill and gave his most famous speech to the Greek world (Acts 17). From Athens they traveled to Corinth, where Paul stayed for two years as a teacher. The Corinthian Christians would also receive at least two letters from St. Paul.

Paul eventually arrived in Ephesus, where he taught for more than two years at Tyrannus Hall, a place reported in some manuscripts to be available for rent during the hours between eleven in the morning and four in the afternoon. This time frame, when slaves were free from their work, became an opportunity for Paul to have interpersonal contact with the highly educated slave population. At this time in Ephesus, it was the slaves who were the teachers for the youth, thereby having an important role in their lives. The long stay at Ephesus meant that Paul and his team personally knew many people in that city of more than 350,000. The book of Acts devotes more space to St. Paul at Ephesus than to time spent in any of the other cities of the Roman Empire.

Luke writes in great detail of several encounters with citizens there, including the near-riot experience at Ephesus's 26,000-person Greek theater (Acts 19, 20, 21). After the incident in the great theater, Paul decided to travel to Rome by way of Jerusalem. En route, he met with elders of the Ephesus believers, who traveled to Miletus and shared their deep affection. Paul knew the people well. "When he had finished speaking, he knelt down with them and prayed. There was much weeping among them all . . . grieving especially because of what he had said, that they would not see him again. Then they brought him to the ship" (Acts 20:36).

## An Ephesian Mystery

*An explanation is warranted.*

With all this history in Ephesus in mind, how do we understand the omission of a list of names at the end of this letter to such close friends? In his closing of Ephesians, Paul names just one person. He writes, "So that you also may know how I am and what I am doing, Tychius will tell you everything. He is a dear brother and a faithful minister of the Lord. I am sending him to you for this very purpose, to let you know how we are, and to encourage your hearts" (Eph 6:21, 22). My suggested answer to the dilemma is simple. If Paul had named individual leaders and close friends in this letter, he might have risked offending those not mentioned.

The absence of a list of names does make the Ephesian letter different from other letters of the apostle, and certain interpreters of Ephesians have been troubled by this omission. Different conclusions have been suggested:

(1) The letter was written later, by a different author than St. Paul. This would mean the letter was written late in the first or second century, by a Pauline group seeking the authority of Paul as author. However, this interpretation contradicts church tradition as well as manuscript evidence that favors the dating of Ephesians prior to 70 AD. As stated by William F. Albright, noteworthy modern archeologist, "We can already say emphatically that there is no longer any solid basis for dating any book of the New Testament after AD 80."[1]

I favor the opinion that all New Testament books were written prior to this date, which marks the destruction of Jerusalem by the Romans.

(2) However, the strongest internal evidence establishes Paul as the author of Ephesians. This view is supported by Markus Barth, interpreter of Ephesians.

> These and other arguments are piled up against the authenticity of Ephesians. They have, for some interpreters, considerable evidential weight, and they have produced wild chases and fanciful suggestions for alternative authors and addressees. Yet none of these suggestions convey any feeling of certainty. It is still possible to hold that Paul is the author of Ephesians; all theories created for showing a different author raise more problems than they solve.[2]

I have been much influenced by one of the most distinguished interpreters of Ephesians, theologian and biblical scholar John A. Mackay, who argues:

> The author of this biblical document, in which the nature of God's order is more fully unveiled than anywhere else in Holy Scripture, is St. Paul. We are at present in the midst of a Pauline renaissance. Because of what Paul and his writings have meant in my own life and thought, it is naturally very gratifying to me personally that today his status in the world of critical Biblical scholarship should

---

1. Albright, *Recent Discoveries in Bible Lands*, 136.
2. Barth, *Broken Wall*, 14–15.

be so very different from what it was half a century or less ago, when his strong voice first spoke to me.³

Therefore, I conclude that Paul truly wrote this letter to the Ephesians.

## After Ephesus

*The journey gets complicated because of those who journey with Paul.*

On the way to Rome, Paul was delayed because of a riot in Jerusalem. It erupted possibly as a result of Paul's traveling in the company of two young Ephesian believers, Tychius and Trophimus. Both were Greeks, and both were with Paul in Jerusalem. Rumors spread that a Gentile had entered the holy place of the temple. This caused a public riot (Acts 21). Paul was placed in temporary protective detention by Roman officials during that unrest, and he was held in the residence "prison" at Caesarea by both Felix Antonius (AD 52–60) and Festus Porcius (AD 60–62), who were Roman procurators of Palestine at the time. The detention lasted two years. Paul became restless. The charges against him were religious, made by the high priest's council. Paul, a Roman citizen, therefore appealed to Festus to send him to Rome for a proper Roman trial. That decision led to the near-disastrous shipboard adventure and the shipwreck at Malta (Acts 27). From there, Paul was finally delivered as a prisoner to Rome.

Upon his arrival in Rome, Paul was warmly greeted by the believers. In describing this occurrence in the book of Acts, Luke writes, "Paul was allowed to stay by himself, with the soldier who guarded him" (Acts 28:16). As his time in prison lengthened to two more years, the treatment became more harsh. After the fire in Rome, 64 AD, the emperor Nero focused the blame on the

3. Mackay, *God's Order*, 10.

Christians. In his final prison letter, Paul tells Timothy of the Roman punishment in the arena. "At my first defense no one took my part . . . but the Lord stood by me . . . so I was rescued from the lion's mouth" (2 Tim 4:16, 17). This time in Rome became his final imprisonment.

While Luke captures much of the life of Paul in detail in the Acts of the Apostles, the book ends abruptly. Paul pays a final tribute to his friend in his last letter, "Luke alone is with me . . ." (2 Tim 4:11, 12).

## Part 3: Support and Encouragement

### Paul Writes from Prison in Rome

*The journey ends in Rome, but the message does not.*

DURING THIS TIME IN Rome, Paul wrote some of his most important letters. One of those letters was his letter to the Christians at Ephesus (the longest of his prison letters), as well as a brief companion letter to the believers at nearby Colossae. In the Colossian letter, Paul names not only Tychius and Timothy, who carry the letter, but also sends a wider greeting to other friends in the fellowship at Colossae. He also greets believers in Laodicea and Hierapolis, nearby smaller cities.

Most interpreters of the prison letters of St. Paul have created the following approximate timetable of these letters, near the end of his life. After Timothy delivers a letter to the believers at Philippi, he also delivers a very personal letter to Philemon. The last written document before Paul's death in Rome, sometime after the year 65 of the first century, is 2 Timothy; his young traveling companion received the letter while in Ephesus. In this letter, Paul writes about his companionship with the two young men from Ephesus who had traveled with him and helped him. He writes "I have sent Tychius to Ephesus . . ." (4:12) and "Trophimus I left ill in Miletus" (4:20).

Paul had an amazing ability to make friends throughout his life, and he kept track of their names. For example, in the earlier book, the Letter to the Romans, he devotes an entire chapter to the names of people he personally knows. The list would not offend any. Because Paul never spent time as a resident in Rome proper, he greets groups of people who were highly mobile in the first-century church and knew of him. The list is a fascinating mixture of Jewish and Greek/Roman names, of people with wealth and of slaves Paul had come to know in his travels (Rom 16). New Testament researchers have studied these names and noted the evidence of the amazing and spreading growth of Christian believers and churches in the Mediterranean world.

This movement by a small company of believers, and the message they proclaimed, would endure beyond the collapse of the Roman Empire of Nero.

## Ephesus, a City Paul Loves

*The place that is dear to the heart of Paul.*

The city of Ephesus was very important to Paul. This man of Tarsus would spend more time in Ephesus than in any of the other Mediterranean cities where he traveled. Paul wrote the Letter to the Ephesians from prison in Rome, in the year 65 or 66 of the first century, to believers in Jesus of Nazareth who lived in this ancient city. The people of Ephesus read, treasured, and saved his letter. We, too, read and treasure the letter in our century.

Ephesus lies about 450 miles west from Antioch. Like Antioch, Ephesus was a city on a river—actually two rivers, the Cayster and the Meander—but with a smaller harbor that needed close attention because of a problem with silting. Unlike Antioch, Ephesus was a city highly respected for its culture and tradition throughout the Roman Empire. Ephesus was called a capital city in the south of the Roman province of Asia. Travelers always visited Ephesus en route to Corinth and Rome. The proudest monument in the city was the Grand Temple to Artemis, which was the most impressive (in terms of sheer size) of all Greek temples, with eighty-eight pillars. Each was nineteen meters high. Ephesus gained the title of "Warden of the Temple of Artemis." The temple had burned in 350 BC but was rebuilt on a grander scale, with help from Alexander the Great. Later in the Christian era (around 800 AD, during the Greek Orthodox Church's dominance), the pillars were moved to Constantinople to build the Hagia Sophia Church. The Temple of Artemis is still honored as one of the seven wonders of the ancient world, although only one of the eighty-eight pillars remains today.

The goddess Artemis was pictured as a warrior and also as a fertility goddess. Called "Artemis" by the Greeks, she was renamed "Diana" by the Romans, whose practice was to borrow their gods from the Greeks. An Ephesus industry involved the production of small silver or stone statues of Artemis, and the craftsmen of such wares eventually caused crises for the early believers, including their teacher Paul. The near-riot at the Ephesian theater was in part caused by the guilds of craftsmen who saw the sale of Ephesus's charms declining, and who blamed Paul and the band of believers for the loss of sales. In the account given in the Acts of the Apostles, Luke makes a direct connection. One craftsman is quoted as stating clearly, "You also see and hear that not only in Ephesus, but in almost the whole of Asia, this Paul has persuaded and turned away a considerable number of people, saying that gods made with hands are not gods" (Acts 19:23–41).

The irony of that charge against Paul is that it is not misinformation. The accusation is truthful and accurate, and as a result, a large demonstration of people became angry at Paul and the fellowship of believers in Jesus. Yet Paul does not mention this public scandal in the long letter that he later writes from prison to the Christians in Ephesus, including the very Christians who experienced that opposition by such a large crowd. Perhaps Paul saw that his opponents had, in fact, actually helped to clarify one of the most liberating parts of the whole truth of the gospel of Jesus. Paul's Lord does not need shrines of silver or marble or stone. Perhaps the believers also chose to follow a moderate way of restraint, deciding to wait for the truth—which the silversmith guild leaders had charged as a crime—to sink in and win their hearts to a larger truth. Paul chooses in his letter not to argue against Artemis or her temple, but to allow the fresh air of the discovery of good news to blow freely, as people meet the Lord Jesus, who makes himself known through his grace and truth.

It is to this city, Ephesus, that Paul gives his attention and writes this important epistle. Markus Barth, in his commentary on the book of Ephesians, notes that the importance of this letter is positive, not defensive:

> We are now ready to turn to another positive and enjoyable mark of Ephesians.
>
> The letter to the Ephesians makes no excuses and does not apologize for its existence and character. Its tone is by no means "apologetic."[1]

## Paul Sends Letters to the Churches

*The writings reveal Paul's centered faith and his love for the people.*

If Paul's letter to the Romans is his major book, with its complete telling of the content and meaning of the gospel of Jesus Christ, then Ephesians can be understood as a book about the people of the gospel. The Letter to the Romans presents a vast portrait of the gospel of Jesus Christ. It begins, "For I am not ashamed of the gospel; it is the power of God for salvation to everyone who has faith, to the Jew first and also to the Greek. For in it the righteousness of God is revealed through faith for faith; as it is written; the one who is righteous will live by faith" (Rom 1:16–17).

The six chapters titled the Letter to the Ephesians constitute the longest letter Paul composed during his imprisonment in Rome. This letter, carried to Ephesus by one of their own young believers, Tychius, is addressed to his beloved friends in Christ at

---

1. Barth, *Broken Wall*, 30.

## PART 3: SUPPORT AND ENCOURAGEMENT

Ephesus and begins with a prayer. Just as my breath is taken away when I hear the opening of Romans, so am I profoundly moved and shaped by the closing sentence of his Ephesian prayer. "I pray that you may have the power to comprehend with all the saints what is the breadth and length and height, and depth, and to know the love of Christ that surpasses knowledge, so that you may be filled with all the fullness of God" (Eph 3:18–19).

So now we open the Letter itself.

# Section II

# Paul Reaches Out to the People of the Gospel

*(An Exposition of Ephesians 1–3)*

### The Message that Paul Sends Unfolds as a Prayer

IN THESE CHAPTERS AS Paul focuses on a prayer for the people, he explains the gospel—what it is and what it means. He tells the reader that the gospel is the mystery of Christ's universal love. In this context the man from Tarsus acknowledges the hostility of tribalism that divides. Over and over he confirms that the gospel addresses the dangers of separation and focuses on the truth of God's love for all. He makes clear that salvation is a gift of grace that allows us to be one with God and with each other.

# Part 4: **Belovedness Revealed**

### Ephesians 1:1–14

### Beginning with Grace and Peace

¹ Paul, an apostle of Christ Jesus by the will of God, To the saints who are in Ephesus and are faithful in Christ Jesus: ² Grace to you and peace from God our Father and the Lord Jesus Christ.

³ Blessed be the God and Father of our Lord Jesus Christ, who has blessed us in Christ with every spiritual blessing in the heavenly places, ⁴ just as he chose us in Christ before the foundation of the world to be holy and blameless before him in love. ⁵ He destined us for adoption as his children through Jesus Christ, according to the good pleasure of his will, ⁶ to the praise of his glorious grace that he freely bestowed on us in the Beloved. ⁷ In him we have redemption through his blood, the forgiveness of our trespasses, according to the riches of his grace ⁸ which he lavished upon us ⁹ for he has made known to us the mystery of his will, in all wisdom and insight according to his purpose which he set forth in Christ, ¹⁰ as a plan for the fullness of time, to gather up all things in him, things in heaven and things on earth. ¹¹ In Christ we have also obtained an inheritance, having been destined according to the purpose of him who accomplishes all things according to his counsel and will, ¹² so that we, who were the first to set our hope on Christ, might live for the praise of his glory. ¹³ In him you also, when you had heard the word of truth, the gospel of your salvation, and had believed in him, were marked with the seal

SECTION II: PAUL REACHES OUT TO THE PEOPLE OF THE GOSPEL

of the promised Holy Spirit; <sup>14</sup> this is the pledge of our inheritance toward redemption as God's own people, to the praise of his glory.

---

*The people learn about the source of their redemption.*

---

> 1:1–2 *Paul, an apostle of Christ Jesus by the will of God, To the saints who are in Ephesus and are faithful in Christ Jesus: Grace to you and peace from God our Father and the Lord Jesus Christ.*

THE MAN WHO MET Christ on the road to Damascus identifies himself as the writer of this letter to the saints in Ephesus, and he makes use of the word *hagios* (holy ones/saints) to describe the Ephesian believers in Christ. Paul uses this same word in other greetings as well, in Colossians, 2 Corinthians, Philippians, and Romans. It is a word of honor.

He follows with a sentence of blessing that includes grace, which is an expression of the surprise of love from God. "Grace" has its root meaning in the Greek word *chara*, which is "joy" and, in its longer form *charis*, becomes "grace." He writes his letter in Greek, and uses "peace" (*eirene*), however, either a Greek or a Jewish reader would recognize this as a fulfillment sentence. Love and peace both have their fulfillment from "God our father and the Lord Jesus Christ."

> 1:3-8 *Blessed be the God and Father of our Lord Jesus Christ, who has blessed us in Christ with every spiritual blessing in the heavenly places just as he chose us in Christ before the foundation of the world to be holy and blameless before him in love. He destined us for adoption as his children through Jesus Christ, according to the good pleasure of his will, to the praise of his glorious grace that he freely bestowed on us in the Beloved. In him we have redemption through his blood, the forgiveness of our trespasses, according to the riches of his grace that he lavished on us . . .*

PART 4: BELOVEDNESS REVEALED

---

*God has blessed us through Christ.*

---

The opening word of Paul's Ephesian prayer is "blessed." The word *eulogos* ("good word") is translated in the New Testament as "bless" or in some instances as "praise." It has the same spirit as one of Paul's opening words in Romans, "gospel" (Rom 1:16), which is also an *eu* word: *euangelos*, "good message." In Romans, Paul teaches and guides us through the meanings of the gospel. Here in Ephesians, Paul teaches and guides us as a people of the gospel. We are the blessed people. "Blessed by the God and Father of our Lord Jesus Christ who has blessed us in Christ" (Eph 1:3). Behind the first-century words of the Ephesian text is the profound blessing of the ancient prayer given by God to Moses. "The Lord bless you and keep you; the Lord make his face to shine upon you and be gracious to you; the Lord lift up his countenance upon you and give you peace" (Num 6:24-26). In this Old Testament text, the Hebrew word *shalom* is treasured by the Jewish people.

The blessing reminds his friends at Ephesus of their belovedness and their destiny, rooted in God's decision before the very foundation or creation of the earth and fulfilled in Jesus Christ. In him we have redemption through his blood, the forgiveness of our trespasses, according to the riches of his grace that he lavished on us. That destiny is spoken of in universal language by Paul, and it is experienced beyond the boundaries that we ordinarily know—"he chose us" and "in him we have redemption."

> 1:9-14 *With all wisdom and insight he has made known to us the mystery of his will, according to his good pleasure that he set forth in Christ, as a plan for the fullness of time, to gather up all things in him, things in heaven and things on earth. In Christ we have also obtained an inheritance, having been destined according to the purpose of him who accomplishes all things according to his counsel and will, so that we, who were the first to set our hope on Christ, might live for the praise of his glory. In him you also, when you had heard the word of truth, the*

SECTION II: PAUL REACHES OUT TO THE PEOPLE OF THE GOSPEL

> *gospel of your salvation, and had believed in him, were marked with the seal of the promised Holy Spirit; this is the pledge of our inheritance toward redemption as God's own people, to the praise of his glory.*

---

### There is a mystery in God's plan that involves us.

---

In this key text, Paul makes use of a Greek word *anakephala*, translated as "gathered/held together." He combines the preposition *ana* that means "in the middle of" with the noun *kephala*, which refers to hub/center. This complex word appears also in Romans where it is translated/understood as "capital"—a structure that holds everything together, as in the way the top of the column holds the whole structure together, to highlight the concept that our lives are best "summed up" by loving one another. Here, he explains the true meaning of the Ten Commandments as the covenant of God: "Owe no one anything, except to love one another; for the one who loves another has fulfilled the law. The commandments ... are summed up in this word, 'Love your neighbor as yourself.' Love does no wrong to a neighbor; therefore, love is the fulfilling of the law" (Rom 13:9–10).

In both instances, Paul emphasizes the good news that God gathers every strand of grace by his decision so that we who set our hope on Christ might be encouraged. He claims that the parts of our lives are held together in Christ. And it is the love of Christ that pulls everything together. "In him you also, when you had heard the word of truth, the gospel of your salvation, and had believed in him, were marked with the seal of the promised Holy Spirit, this is the pledge of our inheritance toward redemption as God's own people, to the praise of his glory" (Eph 1:13–14). He uses the unusual second-person pronoun to state that we have a role in the mystery of redemption.

PART 4: BELOVEDNESS REVEALED

# Ephesians 1:15–23

## The Good Surprise

¹⁵ I have heard of your faith in the Lord Jesus and your love toward all the saints, and for this reason ¹⁶ I do not cease to give thanks for you as I remember you in my prayers. ¹⁷ I pray that the God of our Lord Jesus Christ, the Father of glory, may give you a spirit of wisdom and revelation as you come to know him, ¹⁸ so that, with the eyes of your heart enlightened, you may know what is the hope to which he has called you, what are the riches of his glorious inheritance among the saints, ¹⁹ and what is the immeasurable greatness of his power for us who believe, according to the working of his great power. ²⁰ God put this power to work in Christ when he raised him from the dead and seated him at his right hand in the heavenly places, ²¹ far above all rule and authority and power and dominion, and above every name that is named, not only in this age but also in the age to come. ²² And he has put all things under his feet and has made him the head over all things for the church, ²³ which is his body, the fullness of him who fills all in all.

1:15–19 *I have heard of your faith in the Lord Jesus and your love toward all the saints, and for this reason I do not cease to give thanks for you as I remember you in my prayers. I pray that the God of our Lord Jesus Christ, the Father of glory, may give you a spirit of wisdom and revelation as you come to know him, so that, with the eyes of your heart enlightened, you may know what is the hope to which he has called you, what are the riches of his glorious inheritance among the saints, and what is the immeasurable greatness of his power for us who believe, according to the working of his great power.*

---

**May those who know Jesus comprehend the hope and understand the riches of the inheritance given.**

---

## SECTION II: PAUL REACHES OUT TO THE PEOPLE OF THE GOSPEL

The apostle continues to pray first by expressing thanksgiving for these friends, because he has heard of their faith and love. He then shares with them prayers that focus on two needs: wisdom (*sophia*) and revelation (*apocalypsis*). "Wisdom" is about realizing the important meaning that undergirds the way we live—the "why" we do what we do. Revelation connotes the sense of surprise "that breaks in upon us." Paul used this word in Romans 1:17, referring to the gospel of God's righteous character, which has broken through to us. It is sometimes translated "reveal," "disclosure," "uncover by a vision." The word has come into English with the sense of truly startling disclosure.

In Romans 1, Paul uses this word in a dramatic way: "I am not ashamed of the gospel . . . in it the righteousness of God is 'breaking through by surprise' (*apocalypsis*)." Later, he will use this word in the future tense as a conflicting assurance. "I consider that the sufferings of this present are not worth comparing with the glory about to break through to us" (Rom 8:18).

As he writes, Paul is praying that the Ephesian Christians will have the steady wisdom and the amazing breakthrough of God's grace, so that their eyes will be able to see for themselves, and they will understand both with their hearts and minds the hope to which God has called them.

> 1:20-23 *God put this power to work in Christ when he raised him from the dead and seated him at his right hand in the heavenly places, far above all rule and authority and power and dominion, and above every name that is named, not only in this age but also in the age to come. And he has put all things under his feet and has made him the head over all things for the church, which is his body, the fullness of him who fills all in all.*

*The power of Christ is above all rule, authority, power, and dominion.*

## PART 4: BELOVEDNESS REVEALED

Paul combines the mind that knows and the heart that feels. He anchors our hope in the power that defeated death when Jesus was raised up from the dead. That power is greater than any human dominion in this age where we and all other humans live, and in the age to come beyond where we now live. We notice in this part of his prayer that Paul sees a vast landscape beyond what we now know, which enables all who believe in our Lord's redeeming sacrifice on our behalf to receive his grace in the forgiveness of our trespasses. Therefore the power of his victory over death opens our eyes to hope, now and in the future.

# Part 5: **Disruption Occurs**

### Ephesians 2:1–10

### A Dark Valley Visited

¹ You were dead through the trespasses and sins ² in which you once lived, following the course of this world, following the ruler of the power of the air, the spirit that is now at work among those who are disobedient. ³ All of us once lived among them in the passions of our flesh, following the desires of flesh and senses, and we were by nature children of wrath, like everyone else. ⁴ But God, who is rich in mercy, out of the great love with which he loved us ⁵ even when we were dead through our trespasses, made us alive together with Christ—by grace you have been saved— ⁶ and raised us up with him and seated us with him in the heavenly places in Christ Jesus, ⁷ so that in the ages to come he might show the immeasurable riches of his grace in kindness toward us in Christ Jesus. ⁸ For by grace you have been saved through faith, and this is not your own doing; it is the gift of God— ⁹ not the result of works, so that no one may boast. ¹⁰ For we are what he has made us, created in Christ Jesus for good works, which God prepared beforehand to be our way of life.

2:1–3 *You were dead through the trespasses and sins in which you once lived, following the course of this world, following the ruler of the power of the air, the spirit that is now at work among those who are disobedient. All of us once lived among them in the passions of our flesh, following the desires of flesh and senses, and we were by nature children of wrath, like everyone else.*

PART 5: DISRUPTION OCCURS

---

*The way we once lived is described as "disobedient."*

---

THE PRAYER NOW MOVES through a darker valley, in which the Ephesians are reminded of their own behavior of wrong choices and trespasses. Paul includes himself in this picture of wrongness. He uses the word "desire" (*thumas*) and intensifies the word with the prefix *epi*: *Epithumas* means "high-speed desire." This refers to our own desires for goals we want to reach. Now, we have made them totally demanding and intensified. This word, when used in the context of moral behavior, is translated in English as "lust" in 2 Peter 2:10. Paul does not set this word into a sexual context, but uses "runaway desire" as a word to describe any behavior that is unchecked or unrestrained in any way by common sense or common discernment. In his second letter to Timothy, Paul also makes use of the word *epithumas* to refer to youthful political or religious radicalism, even fanaticism. Other texts help us to understand the concerns that Paul is addressing. Let's turn to 2 Timothy.

2 Timothy 2:22–25

*Extremism that Harms*

The words directed to young believers in this text further highlight the dangers of runaway desire, including political and religious zeal. Paul alerts the young men and women to:

> [22] Shun youthful passions and pursue righteousness, faith, love, and peace, along with those who call on the Lord from a pure heart. [23] Have nothing to do with stupid and senseless controversies; you know that they breed quarrels. [24] And the Lord's servant must not be quarrelsome but kindly to everyone, an apt teacher, patient, [25] correcting opponents with gentleness. God may perhaps grant that they will repent and come to know the truth . . .

## SECTION II: PAUL REACHES OUT TO THE PEOPLE OF THE GOSPEL

I can imagine that Ephesian Christians reading these words might remember the riot at the Ephesian theater and recall that calm-headed friends of Paul did finally succeed in slowing down the shouting crowd so that no lasting harm occurred. Second Timothy was, in fact, written by Paul when Timothy was in Ephesus. Receiving Paul's last letter, Timothy would have remembered the silversmith riot, and when he read Paul's words about patience, he would be able to smile.

> *Negative behavior distorts the truth. Followers of Jesus are called "to be gentle with opponents."*

Returning to his words to the Ephesians, this man in Christ has good news for runaway desire (desire intensified) that everyone in every century, even readers in our century who are facing political and religious radicalism, will understand. When we read this Ephesian letter, we also know about the dangers of riots that cause death—sometimes, real death, and sometimes, the deadening effect of wrongness on the lives of those who join in with wrongness. He cautions followers of Jesus not to be quarrelsome. Paul exhorts them to model kindness with the confidence that the Lord will help them to find the truth.

> 2:4–10 *But God, who is rich in mercy, out of the great love with which he loved us even when we were dead through our trespasses, made us alive together with Christ—by grace you have been saved—and raised us up with him and seated us with him in the heavenly places in Christ Jesus, so that in the ages to come he might show the immeasurable riches of his grace in kindness toward us in Christ Jesus. For by grace you have been saved through faith, and this is not your own doing; it is the gift of God—not the result of works, so that no one may boast. For we are what he has made us, created in Christ Jesus for good works, which God prepared beforehand to be our way of life.*

Paul tells of the God who is rich in actual acts of mercy because of love. Therefore, though we may be deadened by our trespasses, we "are made alive together with Christ." Paul points to the sacrifice "out of the great love with which he loves us." This grace, from the kindness shown toward us in Jesus Christ, is what makes us safe. This sentence from St. Paul has proven to be totally memorable for Christian believers ever since the letter was written: "For by grace you have been saved through faith; and this is not of your own doing; it is the gift of God, not the result of works, so that no one may boast." Now we are made ready to *do* good deeds. We are created and given by Christ the kindness of his love, so that we may now share that grace with others as a new way of life.

---

*We live by grace. God has created us to share good works.*

---

Paul's prayer continues to help us remember the wide expanse of God's loving good news.

### Ephesians 2:11–22

#### No Longer Aliens

[11] So then, remember that at one time you Gentiles by birth, called "the uncircumcision" by those who are called "the circumcision"—a physical circumcision made in the flesh by human hands— [12] remember that you were at that time without Christ, being aliens from the commonwealth of Israel, and strangers to the covenants of promise, having no hope and without God in the world. [13] But now in Christ Jesus you who once were far off have been brought near by the blood of Christ. [14] For he is our peace; in his flesh he has made both groups into one and has broken down the dividing wall, that is, the hostility between us. [15] He has abolished the law with its commandments and ordinances, that

he might create in himself one new humanity in place of the two, thus making peace, [16] and might reconcile both groups to God in one body through the cross, thus putting to death that hostility through it. [17] So he came and proclaimed peace to you who were far off and peace to those who were near; [18] for through him both of us have access in one Spirit to the Father. [19] So then you are no longer strangers and aliens, but you are citizens with the saints and also members of the household of God, [20] built upon the foundation of the apostles and prophets, with Christ Jesus himself as the cornerstone. [21] In him the whole structure is joined together and grows into a holy temple in the Lord; [22] in whom you also are built together spiritually into a dwelling place for God.

The prayer continues, admonishing us to "remember" with another part of the wide expanse of God's loving good news.

### The sacrifice of Christ is for all.

2:11–13 *So then, remember that at one time you Gentiles by birth, called "the uncircumcision" by those who are called "the circumcision"—a physical circumcision made in the flesh by human hands—remember that you were at that time without Christ, being aliens from the commonwealth of Israel, and strangers to the covenants of promise, having no hope and without God in the world. But now in Christ Jesus you who once were far off have been brought near by the blood of Christ.*

### Circumcision does not determine who belongs and who doesn't.

Paul squarely faces the dangers of cultural and religious separation, with its exclusiveness theme of identity tradition: the insiders of a chosen circle of promise, who then treat those on the other side of the circle's wall as aliens. In the face of this narrow teaching, which many Greek believers experienced, they needed to know that this hostility is contrary to truth and hope. It is almost like a tribal or cultural way of thinking, instead of the way God sees the Greek and Jewish believers. "But now in Christ Jesus you who were far off have been brought near by the blood of Christ" (2:13).

---

*Discrimination against Jews and against Greek Christians is explained.*

---

The man from Tarsus was well aware of discrimination against Jews, a reality within the Roman world. He knew this firsthand, from his own experiences. When he and Silas were singled out at a civic court in Philippi, instead of Luke and Timothy (who were Greeks), the charge was "these men are disturbing our city; they are Jews and advocating customs that are not lawful for us as Romans to adopt or observe." The crowd joined in attacking them, and the magistrates had them stripped of their clothing and ordered them to be beaten with rods (Acts 16:20–22). On another occasion, in the theater "Alexander [a Jewish leader] tried to make a defense before the people. But when they recognized that he was a Jew, for about two hours all of them shouted in nationalistic mantra in unison, 'Great is Artemis of the Ephesians'" (Acts 19:33–34).

Paul faces the same religious discrimination as he traces the relationship between Jewish and Greek Christians. In so doing, Paul prepares us for the wider fulfillment of the covenant of promise found in the Old Testament. Greeks who believed the gospel promise were treated at that time as outsiders and as aliens by certain Jewish believers. Paul explains the historic reasons for the discrimination present. Jewish members of the family of believers have had a longer journey experience because of birth, location, and family belonging, especially in their participation in the traditions of the Abrahamic sign of the covenant. These believers indicated their personal belonging to the eternal covenant promise of the gospel by making the physical mark of circumcision on the eighth day of a boy's life. Now, as Paul taught the

## SECTION II: PAUL REACHES OUT TO THE PEOPLE OF THE GOSPEL

gospel at Ephesus, a large number of Greek men and women had heard and believed the good news about Jesus. They had been baptized and publicly confessed their trust in the gospel of Jesus, but without the rite of circumcision.

This means that both those who are near to the Old Testament covenant traditions and practices, and those who are far from them, were built then upon the same foundation of the apostles as well as the historic heroes: Abraham, Moses, David, and the prophets. Jesus himself is the cornerstone: in him, the whole structure is joined together. Therefore, the original promise is now fulfilled in the mystery that makes Greeks equal heirs of the promise with Jews.

> 2:14–16 *For he is our peace; in his flesh he has made both groups into one and has broken down the dividing wall, that is, the hostility between us. He has abolished the law with its commandments and ordinances, that he might create in himself one new humanity in place of the two, thus making peace, and might reconcile both groups to God in one body through the cross, thus putting to death that hostility through it.*

---

**God has broken down the wall—the ordinances of the law are non-operative because of a greater presence.**

---

At this point, Paul makes a startling affirmation in the boldest of language. He uses the strong word *kataergo*, which is translated "abolished." The word *erg*, "work as event," should be literally translated with the negative "against" (*kata*). Since *ergo* contains the Greek *erg* meaning "work," the sentence should read that Jesus has made the law non-operative, or "no longer operative in the way it was before."

St. Paul uses this fascinating word *kataergo* four times in the beloved chapter 13 of 1 Corinthians. In each case I prefer to translate it as "non-operative":

## PART 5: DISRUPTION OCCURS

As for prophecies, they become no longer at work when the fulfillment comes—1 Cor 13:8

Knowledge is no longer at work because we only know in part—1 Cor 13:9

The partial will no longer be operative when the complete comes—1 Cor 13:10

Childish ways no longer are operative when I become an adult—1 Cor 13:11

First Corinthians 15:26 offers the most dramatic use of this word to describe the victory of Jesus on the cross: "Even death is no longer operative." Death itself has met its match in Jesus. On Good Friday Jesus really died, but death could not hold him. Note, in St. Peter's day of Pentecost sermon and from the apostle Paul, "Death could not hold him" (Acts 2:24) and "God has put all things in subjection under his feet" (1 Cor 15:26–27).

The apostle is saying that the law, now in its fulfillment by Christ, is not at work as it was before, with the religious practice of circumcision as a permanent requirement. Now, God has created a new humanity in place of tribes that were marked and kept separate from each other. Jesus has himself absorbed the hostilities that caused people to see each other as enemies. Because of Jesus we are no longer strangers, but citizens together in the household of God.

The wall of separation that was created by the issue of circumcision, dividing the Greek and Jewish believers, has been broken. In the midst of walls that opposing tribes build, the answer is for each side to gratefully recognize and to know that the cure is in the gospel of Jesus Christ. Paul helps us to hear that healing can happen when we discover the ancient promise, now wonderfully fulfilled. "So then you are no longer strangers and aliens but you are citizens ... and also members of the household of God" (Eph 2:19). Jesus Christ himself is the cornerstone (Eph 2:20). The centered trust in Jesus took over to bind them together.

SECTION II: PAUL REACHES OUT TO THE PEOPLE OF THE GOSPEL

## *Baptism addresses the issue of identity and confirms the promise.*

I believe that here, in St. Paul's helpful explanation of the circumcision crisis of the early church, there is a healing interpretation of the Old Testament tradition for the young New Testament church. Circumcision happens in a boy's life before that boy can participate with his own faith, and yet, it is a covenant of identity and promise. As the young boy grows up, he becomes the man who later confirms the promise, when he takes on the law with his own commitment. Similarly, the baptism of infants, both boys and girls, has been seen from the time of the early church as a covenant of both promise and identity, since an infant receives his or her Christian name at baptism. Like circumcision, it happens in infancy; still, it happens because of the parents' faith. In baptism, my parents claimed the promise in prayer and on my behalf, but as an infant I did not yet respond in faith. Later, in confirmation as a young believer, I made my own confession of faith. Paul's words in the Colossian letter show that baptism spiritually fulfills the "identity intent" of circumcision, as marking the moment an individual becomes a person blessed by the promise (Col 2:12). This is one of the reasons that most Christian churches in both the Western and Eastern traditions have practiced the baptism of infants and young children.

In Baptist church tradition, baptism is interpreted as "believers' baptism." The family of an infant receives a prayer of blessing from the church as a sign of promise and preparation. Then, at the age of his or her own decision-making, the young believer via a personal confession of faith in Jesus Christ receives baptism, usually by immersion. There are also Christian families in traditional churches that choose to prepare their children for baptism at a later time, when the young believers can answer their own faith questions.

PART 5: DISRUPTION OCCURS

# Ephesians 2:17–22

## Remembering the Promise

Paul, in his prayer, now thanks the Lord for men and women who were once far off but have now been brought near by the blood of Jesus Christ. This means that Jesus Christ himself is the one who has "broken down the dividing wall." Because of his death on a Roman cross, he has proclaimed "Peace to you who were far off and peace to those who are near" (2:17).

> 2:17–22 *So he came and proclaimed peace to you who were far off and peace to those who were near; for through him both of us have access in one Spirit to the Father. So then you are no longer strangers and aliens, but you are citizens with the saints and also members of the household of God, built upon the foundation of the apostles and prophets, with Christ Jesus himself as the cornerstone. In him the whole structure is joined together and grows into a holy temple in the Lord; in whom you also are built together spiritually into a dwelling place for God.*

What we see happening in this text is Paul drawing us toward the most significant breakthroughs. The reason dividing walls can be broken is that Jesus Christ stands at the center of every human encounter, whether or not we or the others around us fully understand the beloved mediator role of Jesus, who loves us and our neighbor. Jesus is the redeemer who takes upon himself our wrong actions through his sacrifice on the cross; therefore, Christ's act on our behalf brings peace by breaking down the walls with his presence. If we trust and live by this good truth, we can become peacemakers, too—in our neighborhood, city, country, and world.

---

*A person's identity is set by Christ.*

---

Here we encounter the answer of the gospel to the universal longing for human identity, as we seek to know who we are. We are reminded that our basic identity as human beings is rooted in

God's love for us. The good news of this centered trust in Jesus as mediator and savior extends beyond the circumcision controversy that these believers faced. The sheer grace of this belovedness is the primary marker of our identity.

We are the children of God. Our identity in Christ guides our behavior by reminding us of the essential truth that we all are created in God's image and are loved. This truth provides the plumb line for how I view not only myself but also how I view others in my surround, who are beloved, too. This understanding changes the way I make decisions, how I express myself and the manner in which I act towards others. The blessing of belovedness is granted for all people; it is the mystery of Christ. We have become fellow heirs through the gospel. This foundation of belonging liberates us and frees us from prejudice and hatred and unites us as one people.

Jesus Christ is the Lord of all. This explains why Paul is clearly an anti-tribalist. The apostle invites Jewish Christians to welcome all who trust in Jesus Christ. He personally discovered the reconciling peace on the road to Damascus at high noon in the risen Christ. He experienced inclusiveness in the small, persecuted church in Damascus among those who were followers of Jesus. Paul makes it clear that accepting God's love by faith is the basis of covenant identity. This act is the greater foundation whereby to live.

---

*Be careful not to find identity in categories other than our basic identity in Christ.*

---

At this point, Ephesians offers a vitally important resolution from St. Paul. We recognize that there are secondary markers that may crowd up against this primary marker, such as the tribe we associate with, the language we speak, color of our skin, declaration of our race, religious rites we practice, level of education, work we do, our sexual orientation, what church we join, or the obligations and debts we may owe. If I declare (to myself or to others) that my most important identity comes from the school I graduated from, or where my loyalties lie, or my preferences of religious practice, or my political party I can lose perspective and can forget that my primary identity is that I am beloved by God. In so doing, I may find myself veering from the center. Christ has revealed that our identity resides in relationship with him. We do not negate the value of the secondary markers, but we do suggest that we see them as a part of but not the whole expression of meaning of our worth as human beings. However, if I allow a secondary marker to become the prime marker for informing myself or others who I am, I am tempted to shift off center and thereby err in my comprehension of the guiding principle of my being.

As we read these words of Paul today, we recognize the need for his broad and joyous vision of humanity, set free from the loneliness and the false divides of arrogance that create alienation. We can then see for ourselves the real danger of populist movements that support social and ethnic patterns of selective hatreds, false visions of self-greatness, and even conspiratorial visions of people and groups of people who are the supposed enemies of what we think of as our tribe.

These words help us to understand that perceived walls of separation can impact our decisions and actions too quickly, with reference to those we see as either for us or against us. Group alienation as well as solitary estrangement can sometimes join in a dangerous partnership with religion. Religious convictions may then morph into choices that do harm. It was Blaise Pascal who warned that "men never do evil so completely and cheerfully as when they do it from religious convictions."[1]

Because Paul writes to the Ephesians after the debate in the meeting of the council with the elders (discussed in Acts 15:6–19) he is emboldened in this intercessory prayer and reminds his Ephesian readers, most of whom would be Greek, and many of whom may have felt that they themselves were strangers to the covenants of promise—or perhaps, at best, second-class disciples or incomplete disciples—that they are no such thing. He helps

---

1. Pascal, *Pensées*, #894.

us to hear that healing can happen when we discover the ancient promise, now wonderfully fulfilled. "So then you are no longer strangers and aliens but you are citizens ... and also members of the household of God" (Eph 2:19). Jesus Christ himself is the cornerstone (Eph 2:20).

## Colossians 2:11–14

### *Erasing the Record*

To expand on the idea of the meaning of baptism and circumcision, we look at a passage in Colossians. Here we discover that the baptism of a Greek believer fulfills circumcision and "makes us alive together" with Christ.

> [11] In him also you were circumcised with a spiritual circumcision, by putting off the body of the flesh in the circumcision of Christ; [12] when you were buried with him in baptism, you were also raised with him through faith in the power of God, who raised him from the dead. [13] And when you were dead in trespasses and the uncircumcision of your flesh, God made you alive together with him, when he forgave us all our trespasses, [14] erasing the record that stood against us with its legal demands. He set this aside, nailing it to the cross.

---

**Faith in Christ, not rituals or practices, is what defines/leads to fulfillment.**

---

Paul's wisdom and generosity of spirit led to a faithful theological agreement when the first church council meeting at Jerusalem made it clear that faith in Jesus is the true fulfillment of the meaning of the covenants made by God to Abraham and Moses. Therefore, Gentiles who believe the gospel and have faith in Christ do not need physical circumcision. When James, the bishop of Jerusalem, gave his sermon at the first church council, he endorsed

PART 5: DISRUPTION OCCURS

the argument made by Paul, Barnabas, and Peter at that council. We learn in Acts how Luke tells that story.

Acts 15:6–11, 13–14, 19

*The Debate that Ended Well*

The Acts of the Apostles confirms the foundation whereby God has fulfilled the covenant and created a broader definition of who we are "as included in the body of Christ."

> [6] The apostles and the elders met together to consider this matter. [7] After there had been much debate, Peter stood up and said to them, "My brothers, you know that in the early days God made a choice among you, that I should be the one through whom the Gentiles would hear the message of the good news and become believers. [8] And God, who knows the human heart, testified to them by giving them the Holy Spirit, just as he did to us; [9] and in cleansing their hearts by faith he has made no distinction between them and us. [10] Now therefore why are you putting God to the test by placing on the neck of the disciples a yoke that neither our ancestors nor we have been able to bear? [11] On the contrary, we believe that we will be saved through the grace of the Lord Jesus, just as they will." . . . [13] After they finished speaking, James replied, "My brothers, listen to me. [14] Simeon has related how God first looked favorably on the Gentiles, to take from among them a people for his name. [19] Therefore I have reached the decision that we should not trouble those Gentiles who are turning to God . . ."

**The promise of covenant is interpreted and expanded.**

As mentioned earlier, Paul wrote his Letter to the Ephesians after this council described by Luke had been held, but among certain Jewish Christians, there remained the teaching that a truly

SECTION II: PAUL REACHES OUT TO THE PEOPLE OF THE GOSPEL

faithful new believer in the gospel should comply with the ancient Abrahamic tradition of circumcision. This debate is also a major theme in Paul's Letter to the Galatians (see Gal 2:10). The discussion continued among Christians in the first century.

## Acts 21:27–36

### Danger in Jerusalem

In this text recorded by Luke, we have a vivid description of why Paul was arrested and detained for two years at Caesarea, home of the Roman governor. In spite of the circumstances, Paul helps us to understand the inclusiveness for all who believe, which then becomes a major theme in the book of Ephesians.

> [27] When the seven days were almost completed, the Jews from Asia, who had seen him in the temple, stirred up the whole crowd. They seized him, [28] shouting, "Fellow Israelites, help! This is the man who is teaching everyone everywhere against our people, our law, and this place; more than that, he has actually brought Greeks into the temple and has defiled this holy place." [29] For they had previously seen Trophimus the Ephesian with him in the city, and they supposed that Paul had brought him into the temple. [30] Then all the city was aroused, and the people rushed together. They seized Paul and dragged him out of the temple, and immediately the doors were shut. [31] While they were trying to kill him, word came to the tribune of the cohort that all Jerusalem was in an uproar. [32] Immediately he took soldiers and centurions and ran down to them. When they saw the tribune and the soldiers, they stopped beating Paul. [33] Then the tribune came, arrested him, and ordered him to be bound with two chains; he inquired who he was and what he had done. [34] Some in the crowd shouted one thing, some another; and as he could not learn the facts because of the uproar, he ordered him to be brought into the barracks. [35] When Paul came to the steps, the violence of the mob was so great that he had to be carried by the soldiers. [36] The crowd that followed kept shouting, "Away with him!"

PART 5: DISRUPTION OCCURS

---

*Paul preaches inclusiveness and is arrested.*

---

The charge brought against Paul before the high priest was a religious charge. He was held without a final trial before the high priest and council because Roman officials kept him in protective custody for two years. When Agrippa, a Herodian king, visited Festus, the Roman procurator at the Herod estate and harbor at Caesarea (rented from the House of Herod by the Romans, for the governor's residence), Paul was asked to share a part of his story with Agrippa and his wife, and also with Bernice the wife of Festus. "Agrippa said to Festus, 'This man could have been set free if he had not appealed to the Emperor'" (Acts 26:32). For this reason, Festus sent Paul to Rome as a prisoner: because he was a Roman citizen. Therefore, a humorous statement could be made that because of a false rumor about a young Ephesian man, Trophimus, Paul was indeed imprisoned because of his friendship with Ephesian Greeks.

What may seem strange is that Paul rejoices in this imprisonment as he feels that it honors the connection with Greek Christians. It reminds Paul of the mystery that is breaking through by a wonderful surprise. Once again in his prayer, he repeats the dramatic word *apocalypse*. This mystery has broken in upon all humanity, and it is the mystery of Christ that Gentiles are fellow heirs, members of the same body, equally sharing together in the promise of Christ Jesus through the gospel. All of this story is because of the eternal purpose of God.

In Ephesians, both in chapter 2 and again in chapter 3, we are brought into the larger hope of the wide extent of God's grace and truth.

# Part 6: **Grace Intervenes**

### Ephesians 3:1-13

#### Understanding the Promise

¹ This is the reason that I Paul am a prisoner for Christ Jesus for the sake of you Gentiles— ² for surely you have already heard of the commission of God's grace that was given me for you, ³ and how the mystery was made known to me by revelation, as I wrote above in a few words, ⁴ a reading of which will enable you to perceive my understanding of the mystery of Christ. ⁵ In former generations this mystery was not made known to humankind, as it has now been revealed to his holy apostles and prophets by the Spirit: ⁶ that is, the Gentiles have become fellow heirs, members of the same body, and sharers in the promise in Christ Jesus through the gospel.

⁷ Of this gospel I have become a servant according to the gift of God's grace that was given me by the working of his power. ⁸ Although I am the very least of all the saints, this grace was given to me to bring to the Gentiles the news of the boundless riches of Christ, ⁹ and to make everyone see what is the plan of the mystery hidden for ages in God who created all things; ¹⁰ so that through the church the wisdom of God in its rich variety might now be made known to the rulers and authorities in the heavenly places. ¹¹ This was in accordance with the eternal purpose that he has carried out in Christ Jesus our Lord, ¹² in whom we have access to God in boldness and confidence through faith in him.

PART 6: GRACE INTERVENES

¹³ I pray therefore that you may not lose heart over my sufferings for you; they are your glory.

PAUL'S HEALING WORDS CONTINUE as he describes the role of grace that he experienced and his role in proclaiming this grace broadly.

> 3:1–10 *This is the reason that I Paul am a prisoner for Christ Jesus for the sake of you Gentiles—for surely you have already heard of the commission of God's grace that was given me for you, and how the mystery was made known to me by revelation, as I wrote above in a few words, a reading of which will enable you to perceive my understanding of the mystery of Christ. In former generations this mystery was not made known to humankind, as it has now been revealed to his holy apostles and prophets by the Spirit: that is, the Gentiles have become fellow heirs, members of the same body, and sharers in the promise in Christ Jesus through the gospel. Of this gospel I have become a servant according to the gift of God's grace that was given me by the working of his power. Although I am the very least of all the saints, this grace was given to me to bring to the Gentiles the news of the boundless riches of Christ, and to make everyone see what is the plan of the mystery hidden for ages in God who created all things; so that through the church the wisdom of God in its rich variety might now be made known to the rulers and authorities in the heavenly places.*

This paragraph tells of a mystery that unites themes that were proposed in chapters 1 and 2. The word "mystery" appears in three places within these sentences. First, the "*mystery* was made known by revelation." In the second use, a reading "will enable you to perceive my understanding of the *mystery* of Christ." Third, "In former generations this *mystery* was not made known to mankind."

Here, Paul describes the grace present in the household as the result of the great mystery of Christ. This mystery is not for an exclusive and tight circle of especially endowed keepers of tribal secrets, which would have pleased both strict legalists and gnostic philosophers; instead, it is the mystery of the inclusion of Jews and

Greeks and every other language and culture. Paul uses the even larger term, "humankind," *anthropos* (Eph 3:4).

---
*The mystery merits discussion and clarification.*

---

The Greek word *mysterion* is translated as "mystery." It is used often in the sense of a knowledge only known through special, privileged access. This word was often favored in the late first and second century by those who were involved in gnostic or pre-gnostic groups, which became a significant movement in the second through the eighth centuries. In the New Testament books there are signs of pre-gnostic influences, but in each instance, the New Testament writers oppose the gnostic teaching. Readers of the New Testament will notice Paul's opposition to gnostic themes in 1 and 2 Corinthians and also in Colossians, which is a companion letter to his Ephesian letter.

F. F. Bruce, in his commentary on Colossians, especially notes the sentences that challenged pre-gnostic infuences (see Col 2:8–9). Within Ephesians, it is interesting to note Paul's use of this word "mystery." Any gnostic reader who might have been cheered by the appearance of the word "mystery" in chapter 3 would have been gravely disappointed by Paul's explanation of the word. He is not interested in cultic or special themes of a spiritualized Christ, or a Platonic fascination with the philosophic differences between appearance and reality themes that second-century and later gnostic writers promoted using the "mystery" term. Yet "mystery" is important to Paul: It is the mystery of God's love for outsiders, like the Greek believers who trust the Lord Jesus, so that by God's grace their faith is honored. Their inclusion in the beloved family and household of faith is Paul's good mystery.

Gnosticism, at its core, describes the special possession of superior *gnosis*—knowledge that is hidden except for an inner "knowing" circle. Though Jesus is an object of focus in gnostic teaching, he is defined in an especially spiritualized way. This alternate way takes the historical man Jesus of Nazareth away from ordinary history. He is now captured not as Jesus of Nazareth but as the object of an ideology that is friendly to the spiritualized framework of the new "knowing." In Gnosticism, Jesus Christ is therefore not the subject of the sentence of faith, but the object controlled by a new idealism.

In 1945, a large library of third-century gnostic documents were discovered in Nag Hammadi, Egypt. These documents had been part of the Manichaean and gnostic dualism movements that were particularly influential in Persia. This belief constructed an idealized Jesus Christ so wondrously spiritual that the humiliation of the cross was rejected. In gnostic theology, Jesus only "appeared to die" because he was too wondrously powerful for that humiliation. But the spiritualism of the phantom-like Christ is not the true mystery for New Testament believers.

John the disciple, in his first letter, calls out the pre-Gnosticism he saw emerging in certain circles as false teaching (1 John 4:1–3). This means the first heresy called out by the New Testament church was not the denial of the deity of Jesus but the denial of his humanity. We are grateful for the early creeds professing our faith in Father, Son, and Holy Spirit, not least because they insist that the true "good news" is that we worship the Jesus who actually lived among real people, in real places. He is the man Jesus who taught us, suffered on our behalf to take upon himself our sins, and died a real death on the cross. This Jesus rose again from the dead within our human history, and death could not hold him. It is the living Jesus Christ who met Paul on the Damascus road.

## Ephesians 3:14–21

### The Mystery Put to Music

[14] For this reason I bow my knees before the Father, [15] from whom every family in heaven and on earth takes its name. [16] I pray that, according to the riches of his glory, he may grant that you may be strengthened in your inner being with power through his Spirit, [17] and that Christ may dwell in your hearts through faith, as you are being

> rooted and grounded in love. [18] I pray that you may have the power to comprehend, with all the saints, what is the breadth and length and height and depth, [19] and to know the love of Christ that surpasses knowledge, so that you may be filled with all the fullness of God.
>
> [20] Now to him who by the power at work within us is able to accomplish abundantly far more than all we can ask or imagine, [21] to him be glory in the church and in Christ Jesus to all generations, forever and ever. Amen.

Paul's prayer is a petition to the Lord. It is pastorally quiet and totally melodic, even poetic. It is a family prayer, yet wide and even heavenly in its expanse.

> 3:14–19 *For this reason I bow my knees before the Father, from whom every family in heaven and on earth takes its name. I pray that, according to the riches of his glory, he may grant that you may be strengthened in your inner being with power through his Spirit, and that Christ may dwell in your hearts through faith, as you are being rooted and grounded in love. I pray that you may have the power to comprehend, with all the saints, what is the breadth and length and height and depth, and to know the love of Christ that surpasses knowledge, so that you may be filled with all the fullness of God.*

At the same moment, the prayer is tenderly individualized. Paul includes each of us, whom he then draws into a forever family. This is relationship language, personally intense. He treats us as equals, humans who are privileged to know Jesus Christ personally, since by our simple faith he dwells within our hearts.

## *Sanctification discussed.*

Sanctification relates to the fruits of righteousness being shown and expressed in a person's life. Here is the implication: It is not just talking about my faith, but walking with the faith in my life as I relate to others, that gives meaning. Paul moves into the beginning and early steps of the best description of sanctification within our separate lives and within our relationships: "you are being rooted and grounded in love." He teaches a simple and basic sanctification theology. "Rooted and grounded" is a living parable of the Christian's life. It makes time a friend of character development, so that as we grow in age, we may grow in grace. Growth in grace takes time, and therefore time itself is a part of the prayer.

St. Paul prays for the minds as much as for the hearts of the believers in Jesus Christ; he asks the Lord to grant power to our minds, so that we may understand the meanings and intellectual content of the expanding breadth, length, height, and depth of the love of Christ that surpasses knowledge, with a fulfillment that is God's doing.

The large, expanded vision, and its challenge to the believers who receive this Letter to the Ephesians, invites them to share the message of welcome and inclusion. Paul gives this wide and steadying word that lives out the fulfillment prayer of chapter 3: "I pray that, according to the riches of his glory, he may grant that you may be strengthened in your inner being with power through his Spirit, and that Christ may dwell in your hearts through faith as you are being rooted and grounded in love" (Eph 3:16, 17). He then adds, "that you may have the power to comprehend, with all the saints, what is the breadth, and length and height and depth, and to know the love of Christ that surpasses knowledge, so that you may be filled with all the fullness of God" (Eph 3:18, 19). In the final sentences of the prayer, St. Paul shares the results of that true mystery, that ordinary believers may be filled with all the fullness of God and may experience the love of Jesus Christ that surpasses knowledge.

> 3:20, 21 *Now to him who by the power at work within us is able to accomplish abundantly far more than all we can ask or imagine, to him be glory in the church and in Christ Jesus to all generations, forever and ever. Amen.*

Paul's final blessing closes with an ascription of praise that has the same sound as King David's final earthly praise to God

SECTION II: PAUL REACHES OUT TO THE PEOPLE OF THE GOSPEL

(1 Chr 29:10–13), which our Lord also quoted at the close of the prayer he taught us, the "Our Father" prayer. In Jesus's prayer, it is a shortened sentence from David's prayer: "For thine is the Kingdom and the power and the glory forever" (Matt 6:13).

---
*The music that describes the closing of Paul's prayer.*

---

This thrilling close with a final blessing and amen, I believe, has an almost musical feel and quality. The musical, poetic sense of the Ephesian prayer has been noticed by many readers. John A. Mackay especially reflects on this symphonic atmosphere in his commentary:

> This letter is pure music. More than one scholar has noted its musical structure and quality. What we read here is truth that sings, doctrine set to music.... What is certain is that the sequence of ideas is liturgical rather than coldly logical.[1]

It seems like an orchestrated overture that might invite a reader or listener into a vast, larger whole.

Another way to see the prayer is to compare it with a certain stand-alone piano and orchestra concerto that also includes within it the ingredients of a place, time, and life experiences that are profoundly affected by that larger theme.

As I sought to understand and find the meanings in Paul's prayer, I recognized that its grand positive theme is always present, yet in various places it is abruptly interrupted by what might appear as negative themes or even chaotic ones. One of my favorite stand-alone piano concertos came into my mind as "just right," musically, for representing the moods and the almost choral resolution of Paul's prayer.

On February 12, 1924 in Brooklyn, New York, a twenty-six-year-old pianist and composer premiered a concerto for piano and orchestra in what was described as a "jazz idiom." Paul

---

1. Mackay, *God's Order*, 17.

PART 6: GRACE INTERVENES

Whiteman[2] directed the orchestra, and George Gershwin[3] was the composer/pianist. The "Rhapsody in Blue" is a breathtaking and wondrous picture of a quiet, even pastorally gentle grand theme interrupted by abrupt street sounds, car horns, and even harshly strident countermelodies. Even after duels between the piano and orchestra, the whole work becomes a tonal masterpiece. The orchestra and the piano each speak with thrilling authority, and a melody of hope nourishes our minds and throats and teary eyes, so that we feel alive and good and hopeful.

Paul's prayer could fit into this sort of musical mixture, with its peaceful tenderness interrupted by apocalyptic breakthroughs—and although the breakthroughs sometimes seem to sing in a negative key, in time each one is resolved with a good surprise. In Ephesians 1:1–23, we heard a positive pastoral and a wider family theme. Paul is thankful for the faith of the Ephesian friends, who have welcomed into their lives the redemption won for us by Jesus Christ, according to the greatness of God's grace toward us. And then in Ephesians 2:1–3 there is a sudden and abrupt interruption, almost like a countermelody that interrupts the rhapsody with the real power of sins and trespasses, bringing death and deadness. But into this shockwave of fierce danger and rage, a stronger good enters into our story, the Son of Man—Jesus—who because of his love brings a new possibility. We are alerted to the harsh themes of our sinfulness. Paul includes himself in the crisis of runaway desire on our part, a crisis that makes us people of alienation who trespass on others.

A great musical score like "Rhapsody in Blue" moves through sometimes confusing subthemes of street sounds, and even non-harmonic, abrasive, undefined, or even non-traceable mixtures of sound, but then—either slowly or suddenly—brings resolution in the piano alone or the orchestra alone, yet each finding the other.

2. Paul Whiteman (1890–1967), American bandleader and composer, especially famous in the 1920s and 1930s. He was known as the "King of Jazz." His mix of styles led to his debut of Gershwin's "Rhapsody in Blue."

3. George Gershwin (1898–1937), American pianist and composer of both classical and jazz works. He was awarded the Prize for Popular Song in 2007 by the Library of Congress.

## SECTION II: PAUL REACHES OUT TO THE PEOPLE OF THE GOSPEL

This apocalyptic surprise then becomes a theme of sheer grace, especially for those believers who once lived as outsiders but now know of God's grace in Christ, a grace that created a new humanity in this new household of God planted at Ephesus. The interruption of a gentle theme is welcomed. A theme of goodness and resolution becomes totally thrilling. Similarly, St. Paul manages to mix the whole complicated set of real parts of the human story, now seen in the height of the mystery of God's grace.

Paul takes our breath away, and then he invites the readers of his prison letter to simply pray in gratitude to the Lord who made the best parts happen, and who continues to keep the love that caused it all to endure as forever true.

―――― Section III ――――

# Paul Offers Advice for the People of the Gospel

*(An Exposition of Ephesians 4–6)*

### The Appeal to Live a Life Worthy of the Calling

CHAPTERS 4 TO 6 can be best understood as the apostle Paul's encouragement and counsel to his friends at Ephesus as the people of the gospel. He assures them of the steadying Lordship of Jesus Christ. He teaches them about the marks of faithful discipleship in the face of the windy landscape of temptation and false-journey pathways. This discipleship teaching gives practical guidance for these believers, with special attention given to the relationship between parents and their children as well as between children and their parents. The final chapter describes Paul's "whole armor of God"—the characteristics/features of the Christian life that come into play in the mission and mandate to the world for the followers of Jesus.

SECTION III: PAUL OFFERS ADVICE FOR THE PEOPLE OF THE GOSPEL

## Context of Paul's Imprisonment Explained

> *The conditions of Paul's imprisonment set into first century history.*

Following his prayer for the fellowship of believers in Jesus Christ in Ephesus, Paul writes as a prisoner in the Lord. It appears from Luke's final words that Paul was permitted two years under house arrest, living in Rome with the soldier who guarded him. (Acts 28:16–30). A bit of historical background helps us to understand the world in which Paul was imprisoned.

The Emperor of the Roman Empire during this final period in Paul's life was Nero Claudius Caesar Augustus Germanicus. Born in 37 AD, Nero had been adopted as a child by the Emperor Claudius. Nero's mother, Agrippina, had married Claudius in 48 AD, and after Claudius's murder in 54 AD, Nero was named Emperor. For the first five years of Nero's reign he was guided by two brilliant tutors: the philosopher Seneca, and the respected soldier Africanus Burrus. This period of peace was called his "golden" period. But by 59 AD, Nero had discarded these tutors. Instability, narcissism, and paranoia became the defining explanation for the cruelty and sadism of this emperor. Nero died by suicide in June, 68 AD.

Of note is that four years before his death, starting on July 19, AD 64, a nine-day fire destroyed a large part of the city of Rome. Following that fire, Nero "declared" that the Christians were guilty of creating that fire and charged them with arson. Cruel punishments resulted. Many Christians were punished in gladiator games and by lions set loose in the arena. Throughout history the thought has remained that the fire was started really to satisfy the cruelty of one man: Nero. The arena punishments were meant to divert attention away from Nero himself, because many believed he was responsible for the fire. These conditions had an impact on the severity of treatment and harshness of Paul's time in prison.

PART 6: GRACE INTERVENES

*Paul makes friends of the guards during his imprisonment.*

In his Letter to the Philippians, written before the Letter to the Ephesians, we learn the location of Paul's prison in Rome. The one bit of evidence is in his words that it "has become known throughout the whole imperial guard and to everyone else that my imprisonment is for Christ" (Phil 1:12). Paul also gives a second clue: "Greet every saint in Christ Jesus. The friends who are with me greet you. All the saints greet you, especially those of the emperor's household" (Phil 4:21). This reference shows that Paul made friends with guards. We also know he befriended a jailer in Philippi (Acts 16). The word here for the Emperor's guard is *praetorian*, a technical description of troops assigned to the Emperor. We know from archaeological studies that the Emperor's residence had prisoners' cells beneath the ground. Every castle in Europe and in the ancient world had such locations, especially for celebrity or political prisoners.

# Part 7: The Truth of the Gospel Is the Axiom

## Ephesians 4:1–16

### Obligated to Truth

I therefore, the prisoner in the Lord, beg you to lead a life worthy of the calling to which you have been called, [2] with all humility and gentleness, with patience, bearing with one another in love, [3] making every effort to maintain the unity of the Spirit in the bond of peace. [4] There is one body and one Spirit, just as you were called to the one hope of your calling, [5] one Lord, one faith, one baptism, [6] one God and Father of all, who is above all and through all and in all.

[7] But each of us was given grace according to the measure of Christ's gift. [8] Therefore it is said, "When he ascended on high he made captivity itself a captive, he gave gifts to his people." [9] (When it says, "he ascended," what does it mean but that he had also descended, [9] into the lower parts of the earth? [10] He who descended is the same one who ascended far above all the heavens, so that he might fill all things.) [11] The gifts he gave were that some would be apostles, some prophets, some evangelists, some pastors and teachers, [12] to equip the saints for the world of ministry, for building up the body of Christ, until all of us come to the unity of the faith and of the knowledge of the Son of God, to maturity, to the measure of the full stature of Christ. [14] We must no longer be children, tossed to and fro and blown about by every wind of doctrine, by people's trickery, by their craftiness in deceitful

scheming. [15] But speaking the truth in love, we must grow up in every way into him who is the head, into Christ, [16] from whom the whole body, joined and knit together by every ligament with which it is equipped, as each part is working properly, promotes the body's growth in building itself up in love.

## Ephesians 4:1–3

### Steadied by the Gospel

I therefore, the prisoner in the Lord, beg you to lead a life worthy of the calling to which you have been called, [2] with all humility and gentleness, with patience, bearing with one another in love, [3] making every effort to maintain the unity of the Spirit in the bond of peace.

Paul writes to support the Christians in Ephesus and offer ways to guide them in their role as witnesses of Jesus and his teachings.

---

**The mandate for the Christian in the world.**

---

4:1 *I therefore, the prisoner in the Lord, beg you to lead a life worthy of the calling to which you have been called . . .*

The first word Paul uses in this text, is "therefore." My interpretive translation is that the "therefore" refers back to the great prayer in Ephesians 1–3 and means that we should read what follows in light of what was most recently written—the central, thankful assurance of the love of Jesus that surpasses every other verity.

The next words are "I beg you." The New Revised Standard Version text interprets *paracaleto*, as "beg." For me, this seems an odd translation choice. *Paracaleto* is usually translated "encourage," while "beg" implies a sense of desperation in the apostle's request. I prefer the common and more ordinary request word, "encourage." Paul has not exhibited desperation or great stress anywhere in the

SECTION III: PAUL OFFERS ADVICE FOR THE PEOPLE OF THE GOSPEL

Ephesian letter. Looking forward, we find that even his closing sentence of Ephesians is written in a very matter-of-fact tone.

---

*The axiom is that Jesus Christ is the truth. Based on this truth, we are encouraged to live a life that steadies us, and to live as a witness to this truth.*

---

What Paul encourages his Ephesian friends to do actually makes use of a fascinating word, *axios*, translated "worthy" in the text. The Greek word moves directly into Latin as "axiom," which is a scientific and mathematical term borrowed without translation but by what linguists call "transliteration," so that the word we know in English has the recognizable sound of its source language. An "axiom" is a postulate that requires no proof; it has intrinsic truth for the sake of studying the consequences that follow from it. This truth does not need to be authenticated. Paul places this important truth word, *axios*, in the opening sentence of chapter 4. He encourages them to lead a life *worthy* of the name and calling that the Lord has entrusted in and to them.

Paul's use of the anchor word *axios* is key to the truth of the assurance and dependability of the love of Jesus Christ. Because of the Lord's grace and truth, we are able to experience the significance and magnitude of the axiom—the full mystery of St. Paul's prayer. I interpret the sentence then as "I (therefore) a prisoner in the Lord encourage you who receive this letter to lead a life *steadied* (*axios*) by and as a consequence of the truth and assurance of Christ's love." You can use this truth and act on this truth. It is the assurance of the truth and love of Jesus Christ that is the major anchor. People who are grounded in the Greek and Latin languages would understand the implication of this word. The youthful student of physics and mathematics would understand the expanse of the *axiom* of truth and grace.

This is also what John's Gospel announces: "And the word became flesh and lived among us, and we have seen his glory as

## PART 7: THE TRUTH OF THE GOSPEL IS THE AXIOM

the Father's only Son, full of grace and truth" (John 1:14). St. Paul unites his witness to the witness of St. John.

> 4:2, 3 *with all humility and gentleness, with patience, bearing with one another in love, making every effort to maintain the unity of the Spirit in the bond of peace.*

A reader of the Ephesians text will notice in this chapter that Paul makes his case for the steady and true axiom at the center of the gospel of Jesus Christ. He affirms four discipleship virtues that result from that true centering: humility, teachableness, patience, and lifting one another in the love and goodness of the true *axios*. In so doing, he ascribes these four virtues of discipleship character to the steadying permanence of the love of Jesus, "with all humility and gentleness, with patience, helping to lift each other in love." Added together, these virtues create unity of the spirit in the fellowship of believers and the bond of peace.

The first virtue in Paul's list is humility. This is what Dietrich Bonhoeffer called "the view from below."[1] It is discipleship servanthood. The word is literally "lowly," and Paul is making a root-level lowly place for all character formation. His prayer begins small and is formed by the act of rooting our life, as one would root a young plant. Paul uses this lowly word *tapainos* with another character-building word, *prautes*, that is usually translated "meek," as in "Blessed are the meek," found in the third beatitude (Matt 5:5). The Lord proves his intended meaning here when he tells of the reward for the meek in the beatitude: "they will inherit the earth" for being teachable. I have taught the third beatitude with this promise in mind. "Blessed are the teachable ones . . . for they . . ." I have said to students, "Do you want to play your part in solving the problem of global warming? Then study chemistry and forestry and wild land management . . . in other words, learn because when you are teachable, Jesus has promised that 'the teachable ones . . . will inherit the earth.'"

One fascinating feature in the world of classical Greek is that the word translated "meek" is used to refer to a wild animal, such

---

1. Bonhoeffer, *Letters and Papers From Prison*, 17.

as a wild horse, that is trainable. The word implies "teachable." It does not mean "weak," such as in the dismissive expression, "meek and mild." If it means "teachable," then we have a discipleship word suggesting future greatness and skill—as in a horse trained to run at full speed, even in battle. Yet Paul's teaching works so that those who listen understand that meekness goes together with humility.

The next discipleship virtue mentioned is patience. We remember that earlier in this letter, as Paul described the moral and physical dangers of doing wrong, causing deadness as a result (Eph 2:1–3), he used the strong negative word *epithumia*, "runaway, excessive desire." The wrongness that is *thumas* (desire) is accelerated by the intensified *epi*. Now he uses that same word "desire," but in this text, his prefix word is *makrothumia*, which means to take a long view toward our desire. Paul does not eliminate or "seek to destroy" desire in the human mind or heart, but now he places a time restraint that becomes healthy for the human personality. Desire and ambition are normal, but they need to fit within a large framework of goodness and truth. He calls that framework "patience," which means taking the long view toward all desire.

The fourth virtue is, literally, to "lift up" a friend in order to encourage that friend (or neighbor). The same word is used following the transfiguration scene, where a small group of disciples experience an amazing and overwhelming moment with Jesus (Matt 17:7). The result is that they fall to the ground in fear. The Lord Jesus, we are told in this account by Matthew, comes and helps them stand up. The importance of lifting up another person is now a virtue in Paul's list. Because of the steadying love of Jesus, we now can and should help one another to stand up. These virtues have the power to bring us closer together, into a unity blessed by the Holy Spirit and made real to us through the united oneness of the followers of Jesus Christ: one body, one spirit, one hope, one Lord, one faith, one baptism, one God and Father of all.

PART 7: THE TRUTH OF THE GOSPEL IS THE AXIOM

## Ephesians 4:4-10

### Oneness Not Separateness

> [4] There is one body and one Spirit, just as you were called to the one hope of your calling, [5] one Lord, one faith, one baptism, [6] one God and Father of all, who is above all and through all and in all. [7] But each of us was given grace according to the measure of Christ's gift. [8] Therefore it is said, "When he ascended on high he made captivity itself a captive; he gave gifts to his people." [9] (When it says, "He ascended," what does it mean but that he had also descended into the lower parts of the earth? [10] He who descended is the same one who ascended far above all the heavens, so that he might fill all things.)

In this text, Paul encourages each follower of Jesus to see his or her own mandate alongside the mandate of brothers and sisters who also trust in Jesus. Therefore, he uses an analogy of the human body to describe how we relate to each other. Earlier, he used a different analogy of our common unity, the household of God. The analogy of the household of God presented a structure built upon the foundation cornerstone, and that common stone is the living person Jesus Christ (Eph 2:19–22).

> 4:4-7 *There is one body and one Spirit, just as you were called to the one hope of your calling, one Lord, one faith, one baptism, one God and Father of all, who is above all and through all and in all. But each of us was given grace according to the measure of Christ's gift.*

In chapter 4 we are now pictured as members of a living body of Christ, one body and one spirit. Notice the repetitious use of the number "one." This oneness is not lonely separateness from one another but actually is an understanding of who we are in the opposite direction; Paul teaches unity, not isolated separateness. We conclude that the parts of the body are enriched by the brothers and sisters in our surroundings as we enrich the whole in the bond of peace.

SECTION III: PAUL OFFERS ADVICE FOR THE PEOPLE OF THE GOSPEL

## *Called to follow as individuals, and called to serve together.*

It is instructive to give attention and trace the uses of "one" in the light of Paul's unity conclusion: "One body, one spirit, one hope of our calling, one Lord, one faith, one baptism, one God and Father of all." Note that while Paul points to the assembly of the parts of one, he does not ignore our individuality in receiving grace and gifts from Christ; rather, he envelops the individuality in the call for unity. This analogy is also clearly stated by Paul in the letter to the Corinthians: "There are varieties of gifts, but the same Spirit, and there are varieties of services, but the same Lord, and there are varieties of activities, but it is the same God who activates all of them in everyone. To each is given the manifestation of the Spirit for the common good" (1 Cor 12:4–7).

The sacrament of baptism illustrates this common theme.

### Acts 9:17–19

#### *Baptism Happens in the Fellowship*

Although baptism is singular, received personally and individually, baptism takes place in the surround of the followers of Jesus. We remembered that St. Paul himself was baptized by a fellowship of believers in Damascus, as recorded:

> [17] So Ananias went and entered the house. He laid his hands on Saul and said, "Brother Saul, the Lord Jesus, who appeared to you on your way here, has sent me so that you may regain your sight and be filled with the Holy Spirit." [18] And immediately something like scales fell from his eyes, and his sight was restored. Then he got up and was baptized, [19] and after taking some food, he regained his strength. For several days he was with the disciples in Damascus . . .

## PART 7: THE TRUTH OF THE GOSPEL IS THE AXIOM

Paul does not refer to baptism in any other part of Ephesians. He does offer a major teaching on the meaning of baptism in his Letter to the Colossians, which is the companion book to Ephesians. We can look to Colossians to see how Paul establishes that baptism is for both the individual and for the community, who share the promise for the individual together. Baptism replaced the physical act of circumcision in the early church, thereby fulfilling the ancient covenant of promise first made to Abraham to be blessed and to become a blessing.

---

**Baptism accepts that life is a gift from the Lord and aligns one with the presence and purpose of the Lord.**

---

### Colossians 2:8–15

*Understanding More About the Place of Baptism*

[8] See to it that no one takes you captive through philosophy and empty deceit, according to human tradition, according to the elemental spirits of the universe, and not according to Christ. [9] For in him the whole fullness of deity dwells bodily, [10] and you have come to fullness in him, who is the head of every ruler and authority. [11] In him also you were circumcised with a spiritual circumcision, by putting off the body of the flesh in the circumcision of Christ; [12] when you were buried with him in baptism, you were also raised with him through faith in the power of God, who raised him from the dead. [13] And when you were dead in trespasses and the uncircumcision of your flesh, God made you alive together with him, when he forgave us all our trespasses, [14] erasing the record that stood against us with its legal demands. He set this aside, nailing it to the cross. [15] He disarmed the rulers and authorities and made a public example of them, triumphing over them in it.

SECTION III: PAUL OFFERS ADVICE FOR THE PEOPLE OF THE GOSPEL

> *Baptism is both a personal and an inclusive sign of God's grace.*

Again, notice that Paul interprets baptism as the true fulfillment of circumcision, as a sign of the promise covenant of Abraham. He interprets baptism as "spiritual circumcision" for these Greek believers. The church as the followers of Christ is given instruction from the Lord that includes baptism in the Great Commission. Baptism is given as a sign that points to the presence and authority of Christ: "Now the eleven disciples went to Galilee, to the mountain to which Jesus had directed them. When they saw him, they worshiped him; but some doubted. And Jesus came and said to them, 'All authority in heaven and on earth has been given to me. Go therefore and make disciples of all nations, baptizing them in the name of the Father and of the Son and of the Holy Spirit, and teaching them to obey everything that I have commanded you. And remember, I am with you always, to the end of the age'" (Matt 28:16–20).

> *We are to understand the purpose in Christ's presence on earth, his death and his resurrection.*

> 4:8–10 *Therefore it is said, "When he ascended on high he made captivity itself a captive; he gave gifts to his people." (When it says, "He ascended," what does it mean but that he had also descended into the lower parts of the earth? He who descended is the same one who ascended far above all the heavens, so that he might fill all things.)*

At this point, Paul reminds the reader of Christ's identification with every man and woman, and of the sacrificial victory over sin/death on humanity's behalf. The apostle makes reference to a psalm that expresses the triumph David felt because of God's help in battle (Ps 68:17, 18). The psalm offers praise for the ascending height of God's help. But Paul gives a contrasting meaning to the triumphant part of David's song. Paul states that Christ not only ascended to reign with his Father, but he also descended in saving sacrifice. We now see both the act of the ascension and the descension brought together as the fulfillment of the sacrifice at the cross. It was the singular Jesus who disarmed death and the power of our sins, and the power of all that is evil. In so doing he took on our sinfulness. Jesus absorbed that which held us captive. We saw this lowly Jesus earlier in Ephesians: "But now in Christ Jesus you who were far off have been brought near by the blood of Christ. For he is our peace" (Eph 2:13–14).

Next Paul moves on to discuss separate gifts, which recognize separateness but always point toward a result of unity and wholeness together.

---

*Gifts from the Lord are given on our behalf.*

---

## Ephesians 4:11–14

### Advice for the Road

> [11] The gifts he gave were that some would be apostles, some prophets, some evangelists, some pastors and teachers, [12] to equip the saints for the work of ministry, for building up the body of Christ, [13] until all of us come to the unity of the faith and of the knowledge of the Son of God, to maturity, to the measure of the full stature of Christ. [14] We must no longer be children, tossed to and fro and blown about by every wind of doctrine, by people's trickery, by their craftiness in deceitful scheming.

Paul makes this positive affirmation of the unity of the body in Christ and our own individual growth in grace and maturity.

---

*People have been given a variety of gifts to help them shape and support the body of the followers of Jesus.*

---

## SECTION III: PAUL OFFERS ADVICE FOR THE PEOPLE OF THE GOSPEL

> 4:11–13 *The gifts he gave were that some would be apostles, some prophets, some evangelists, some pastors and teachers, to equip the saints for the work of ministry, for building up the body of Christ, until all of us come to the unity of the faith and of the knowledge of the Son of God, to maturity, to the measure of the full stature of Christ.*

This fourth chapter of Ephesians offers an encouraging list of virtues that are given to individuals to build up the body of Christ. At the same time, these gifts are given to unite the believers and grow their discipleship as Christians. As a caution, Paul then offers a list of alerts to the members of this united fellowship.

*Devious elements exist that threaten the advance of the gospel.*

> 4:14 *We must no longer be children, tossed to and fro and blown about by every wind of doctrine, by people's trickery, by their craftiness in deceitful scheming.*

Note the practical warnings that Paul explains as an equipping alert for those who believe in Christ. Paul offers discipleship words of shrewd advice. He warns against three distractions and temptations disciples face.

*Watch out for distortions of truth.*

Let us pay close attention so as to recognize the alerts as they present themselves. The first warning makes known that there are various winds representing contrasting doctrines and teachings that blow into our entire being. We might be thrown off course, like children who are caught off balance by stormy wind gusts. When this happens, it can affect our ability to think clearly in the face of competing dogmas.

Paul advocates the practical exercise of our minds in learning the truth, therefore keeping us able to test the claims of new but

## PART 7: THE TRUTH OF THE GOSPEL IS THE AXIOM

sometimes exotic teachings (winds) that could confuse and lead us away from the *axios* of truth and grace.

---
*Forces exist that threaten truth.*

---

The second is also a streetwise, commonsense protective alert. Paul draws upon our imagination to suggest tricksters who disorient us, like dice players on the street corner who are all too friendly but turn out to tell secret and hidden truths that are too good to be true—and they do turn out to be too good to be true. The Greek word Paul uses here is a gambler's word, *kubeia*. It is literally the first-century word "dice." We should not be tricked into wrong, hasty, or impulsive decisions that confuse. The translators of the New Testament into English were challenged by the best way to explain this odd, non-theological word, *kubeia*.

The word "dice" appears only in this place in the whole of the New Testament. Paul shows his own seasoned wisdom, and the life experiences of his young adult years, even as he humorously warns these young Ephesian Christians to be prepared for crafty opponents of truth.

It is useful in the expositional understanding of a biblical text to try to understand what the writer (here, St. Paul) is communicating from the total context of the particular sentence. In every culture, we have examples of skillful tricksters who—perhaps with dice or perhaps with words—use tricks to lead a traveler astray. Everyone has personal stories of such experiences, of contests where falsehood is advocated with a sleight of hand. Either on city streets or in our era of Twitter and other online sites, our watchfulness must follow his word of caution to keep our sense of balance in a windy place.

It is instructive for a Bible reader to see how a sentence with unusual word usages is translated for us in different versions of the Bible. We see how each translator seeks to best understand, and present in current English usage, the sentence and its meaning as

SECTION III: PAUL OFFERS ADVICE FOR THE PEOPLE OF THE GOSPEL

it appears in the original text. Let us then see verse 14 of chapter 4 of Ephesians as translated in different versions of this text:

| | |
|---|---|
| James Moffatt, *A New Translation of the Bible*, 1922 | "Blown from our course and swayed by every passing wind of doctrine, by the adroitness of men who are dexterous in devising error" |
| *New International Version*, 2005 | "Every wind of teaching and by the cunning and craftiness of people in their deceitful scheming" |
| *New American Bible*, 1971, Roman Catholic Version | "That originates in human trickery" |
| *New Revised Standard Version Bible*, 1989 | "by people's trickery, by their craftiness" |
| *Jerusalem Bible*, 1966, Roman Catholic Version | "At the mercy of all the tricks men play and their cleverness in practicing deceit" |
| *New English Bible*, 1961 | "dupes of crafty rogues and their deceitful schemes" |
| Authorized Edition *King James Bible*, 1909 | "by the sleight of men and cunning craftiness" |
| Msgr. R.A. Knox, *The New Testament A New Translation*, 1943, Roman Catholic Version | "No longer to be children, to be like storm-tossed sailors, driven before the wind of each new doctrine that human subtlety, human skill in fabricating lies, may propound" |
| Eugene Peterson, *The Message*, 1993 | "No prolonged infancies among us please . . . small children are an easy mark for imposters" |

PART 7: THE TRUTH OF THE GOSPEL IS THE AXIOM

*Knowing what/who to trust is critical and requires careful examination.*

Paul's third alert actually makes use of the word "deceive": We are to beware of "craftiness in deceitful scheming." In this warning, Paul makes use of a word used extensively in the New Testament. He brings in the idea of that which is untrustworthy and fraudulent as he adds *planeo* into the conversation to bring the threats into focus.

Unlike the reference to "dice," we have no translation problems with this Greek word *planao*, meaning "to lead astray." It translates "deceitful." There are sixty-nine uses of this word in the New Testament. It is used by John in his first letter: "If we say we have no sin, we *deceive* ourselves" (1 John 1:8). Paul uses it in his second letter to Timothy, "wicked people . . . will go from bad to worse, deceiving others and being *deceived*" (2 Tim 3:13).

The word *planao* has an interesting companion use in the Greek language, especially as a scientific word in ancient astronomy. We know that before the scientific proof of Nicolaus Copernicus (1473–1543), almost all ancient astronomers assumed that the earth was the center reference point for understanding the earth, the skies, and the heavenly bodies, as part of our total created existence. But even that essential mistake, which for that era explained the sun's reliable journey around the earth each day, left ancient Greek astronomers dissatisfied and baffled by other lights they found in the sky. Some of the "stars," especially ones that humans attached names to like Venus, Mars, and Jupiter, tended to wander in the sky relative to the other stars. The non-wandering stars, and the groups of stars that surrounded them, were also given mythical names. Furthermore, they twinkled. Like the "Big Dipper" group of stars, pointing to the north star—and in the southern hemisphere, the "Southern Cross"—they were less romantic but far more useful. Sailors in the Mediterranean or Atlantic could guide their ships by the north star, but not by Venus or Mars. Therefore, these ancient astronomers named the wandering stars with the Greek word for "wanderers," *planeo*—hence "planet."

Soon, by the time of Aristotle and the philosophers, these wanderers were described as "deceivers." This helps us to understand the origin of the word used in first-century Greek for "deceive." The deceiving stars—the planets—wander, and they do not twinkle. A sea captain cannot guide a ship at sea relative to their position in the sky, because they wander. The real stars, then, are the ones that stay put and twinkle.

As Paul brings the teaching full circle, completing the list of alerts and adding *planeo* to the conversation, I would like to suggest a "spoof" parable of a shifty sea captain who tells us all to jump on board his ship named *Mystery II*, which he tells us in writing is supposedly set to sail to "Barcellona, Spain"—misspelled, which should have been a clue! This captain goes on to announce cheerfully that he will use the "star" Venus as his guide for navigation. Of course, Venus is not a star but a planet. He gives further promises of treasures we have always desired and the best food, too. We can understand that Paul's list of alerts is a similar compilation of wily disinformation.

As a man in Christ, Paul alerts us to trust the north star, which is its own source of light, instead of the planets that borrow or reflect light (like the moon) from our star, the sun. Here, Paul makes light the equivalent of truth, the *axios*—intrinsic light that can be trusted. The New Testament gospel has, because of God's revelation and by apocalyptic breakthrough, made known the eternal truth and grace that radiates from Jesus Christ. When we discover and follow that light, we can find our way, and in that finding know our own belovedness too, because "in him was life, and the life was the light of all people" (John 1:4).

Paul follows the discourse on the importance of being aware of that which distracts and distorts the truth, giving us a sentence of sheer goodness and hope. After the three alerts, Paul puts the *axios* truth theme together with the eternal love theme.

PART 7: THE TRUTH OF THE GOSPEL IS THE AXIOM

## Ephesians 4:15–16

### A People Equipped

> [15] But speaking the truth in love, we must grow up in every way into him who is the head, into Christ, [16] from whom the whole body, joined and knit together by every ligament with which it is equipped, as each part is working properly, promotes the body's growth in building itself up in love.

---

***Followers of Christ are expected to be equipped and work together in an arrangement that best serves the Lord.***

---

> 4:15 *But speaking the truth in love, we must grow up in every way into him who is the head, into Christ . . .*

Here the reference to Jesus Christ as the head of the body is clear. This image appears earlier with the words, "God made Jesus Christ the head over all things for the church" (Eph 1:22). It also appears where the Lord is described as "He is before all things, and in him all things hold together. He is the head of the body, the church; he is the beginning, the firstborn from the dead, so that he might come to have first place in everything" (Col 1:17).

> 4:16 *. . . from whom the whole body, joined and knit together by every ligament with which it is equipped, as each part is working properly, promotes the body's growth in building itself up in love.*

Paul makes fascinating word choices. In this text he makes use of two intriguing words.

One, *synarmologeo*, is used earlier (Eph 2:21). It is an engineering word. It means "structure put together for a reason in a place." Like many technical Greek terms, it has an almost humorous and complicated derivation. It starts as *syn*, "with." The second part of the word is *arma*, which is the noun "chariot." The third part of the word is *meno*, "place." The last part of the word

77

is *logos*, which means "meaningful." Therefore, this technical term, made up of individual parts, is a union of "with," "chariot," "place," and finally "meaning."

Those who translated this odd long word gave us, as written earlier, "In him the whole structure is joined and knit together and grows into a holy temple in the Lord" (Eph 2:21). In his description of the household of God, Paul tells us that the structure is a single entity, one body.

> *Followers of Christ are advised to hold together, to be connected.*

The man from Tarsus then repeats this same word in Ephesians 4:16. Here, the NRSV translators offer us the English: "From whom the whole body, *joined and knit together* . . ." Notice that back in Ephesians 2:21, Paul is describing believers in Christ as a household of God, and we are integral parts of that building, "a building as it is built." Now, he is describing a believer in Christ as a living part of the body of Christ. In each case, the apostle makes use of the same word, first in an engineering context and then in an anatomical sense.

Both words have the "meaning" word *logos* at their core. This means that each text describes the "chariot" as meaningful, and also with *meno*, "place," which means that each is planted on earth. We are to be like a temple in a place, like a building, and then in chapter 4 we are to be like a human person's body. In other words, it is Jesus Christ who is the foundation upon which the home stands, and in this fourth chapter, Jesus Christ is the head of the body. In both references, the place is here on earth.

But there is one more fascinating word that Paul adds to the house and the living body. He adds this word to the first part of the sentence. Paul tells us that the body is joined together, but he then adds the word that gives us our English text translation, "knit together by every ligament with which it is equipped as each part is working properly, promotes the body's growth in building itself up in love." The word translated "knit together" is a musical term, *epichoregia*. The root of the word is "chorus," as in a choir or singing group, or even "choreograph"—creating dance steps to go with the music.

Paul also uses this word when he thanks the Philippians for their prayers on his behalf while he is in prison in Rome. He writes, "I know that through your prayers and the *help* of the Spirit of Jesus Christ this will turn out for my deliverance" (Phil 1:19). The word translated "help" in this text is this same word he uses now in Ephesians 4. Paul is saying, "Through your prayers and the *choreography* of the Spirit of Jesus Christ, I will be blessed." This becomes an important theological understanding of the mystery and vital role of our prayers. The prayers of his friends at Philippi work together in concert and are seen by Paul as part of his deliverance experience.

Paul is, in fact, saying that Jesus Christ is choreographing our individual parts in his church, the body of Christ. He puts every part, even ligaments, together because of his love for us. In his choreographing of our lives, he honors who we are and the uniqueness we each have. He is like the expert choral director who knows the notes of our range and even our special giftedness at songs or dances. He helps us find where we will fit into the chorus in a way that honors each singer or musician best, as it honors the whole chorale. Paul also wants us to know that it is in the working together that we encourage the whole as individuals and further the purpose of our calling.

## Ephesians 4:17–19

### Pay Attention

> [17] Now this I affirm and insist on in the Lord: you must no longer live as the Gentiles live, in the futility of their minds. [18] They are darkened in their understanding, alienated from the life of God because of their ignorance and hardness of heart. [19] They have lost all sensitivity and

have abandoned themselves to licentiousness, greedy to practice every kind of impurity.

The gist of these sentences is almost as if Paul now plays the role of a coach or trainer, with practical moral and discipleship guidance. He is an older and experienced disciple, helping younger members of the Christian fellowship at Ephesus to navigate the challenges of their daily living in the Roman world at the midpoint of the first century. Paul respects these believers, which is a positive starting point in his thankful recounting of their love for each other and their growing spiritual giftedness as members of the body of Christ.

> 4:17 *Now this I affirm and insist on in the Lord: you must no longer live as the Gentiles live, in the futility of their minds.*

The apostle offers guidance and advice that he signals as urgent by the use of the strong word *marturomen*. The English translators show this urgency by using the word "insist" in the NRSV text. This word is generally translated in the New Testament as "witness," but the Greek word has come into English as the grim word of heroic deaths, "martyr." The word means "heavy-weighted witness, as in a time of urgency." Paul narrates a journey or pathway of moral and spiritual decline, which could happen for and within these young Christians in Ephesus if they lose their trust in the *axios*, the steadiness of God's truth and love in Jesus Christ.

---

**Futility is not an option.**

---

This sentence is clear: "I witness this to you in love." Paul as a guide cautions his friends at Ephesus against living day by day in a way that he describes as "in the futility of their minds." His word for "futile" is *mataios*, which means "transitoriness" or "of no consequence." Its source comes in part from a dualistic and often cynical worldview that was present in certain first-century Greek and Roman philosophers, a no-consequence outlook on life choices and behavior. It sees our daily life and the people who surround us as boundaried by that transitoriness.

St. Paul uses this same word *mataios* when writing to the Romans to declare that transitoriness is not the last word.

## Romans 8:18–25

*Fulfillment by God's Decision*

---

**What we experience in the present does not compare to what we will experience in the future.**

---

> [18] I consider that the sufferings of this present time are not worth comparing with the glory about to be revealed to us. [19] For the creation waits with eager longing for the revealing of the children of God; [20] for the creation was subjected to futility, not of its own will but by the will of the one who subjected it, in hope [21] that the creation itself will be set free from its bondage to decay and will obtain the freedom of the glory of the children of God. [22] We know that the whole creation has been groaning in labor pains until now; [23] and not only the creation, but we ourselves, who have the first fruits of the Spirit, groan inwardly while we wait for adoption, the redemption of our bodies. [24] For in hope we were saved. Now hope that is seen is not hope. For who hopes for what is seen? [25] But if we hope for what we do not see, we wait for it with patience.

Paul uses the image of "groaning in labor pains" to describe what we experience now. It is transitory—it will pass. Labor does pass and end with the miracle of life. We are not aware of the dimensions or features of that life until it makes itself known. It is made clear that hope goes beyond what we can see, and it calls us to live in hope for what we cannot see. The apostle presents the long view and gives assurance that "in hope we were saved."

SECTION III: PAUL OFFERS ADVICE FOR THE PEOPLE OF THE GOSPEL

*We do not see nor know all that is ahead of us.*

While we are limited, the Lord's view exceeds all boundaries. Paul makes clear that the present is not permanent. He challenges this fatalistic boundary of transitoriness with his affirmation of the fulfillment proclaimed in the gospel, which tells of a destiny for the whole creation because of the events on Good Friday and Easter. We see ourselves and the whole creation in that thrilling light. In Romans, we are given words that settle us.

*There is staying power in recognizing that hope goes beyond our comprehension.*

Romans 8:31–39

*A Sure Victory*

The last word belongs to the love of God in Christ Jesus our Lord.

> [31] What then are we to say about these things? If God is for us, who is against us? [32] He who did not withhold his own Son, but gave him up for all of us, will he not with him also give us everything else? [33] Who will bring any charge against God's elect? It is God who justifies. [34] Who is to condemn? It is Christ Jesus, who died, yes, who was raised, who is at the right hand of God, who indeed intercedes for us. [35] Who will separate us from the love of Christ? Will hardship, or distress, or persecution, or famine, or nakedness, or peril, or sword? [36] As it is written, "For your sake we are being killed all day long; we are accounted as sheep to be slaughtered." [37] No, in all these things we are more than conquerors through him who loved us. [38] For I am convinced that neither death, nor life, nor angels, nor rulers, nor things present, nor things to come, nor powers, [39] nor height, nor depth, nor

## PART 7: THE TRUTH OF THE GOSPEL IS THE AXIOM

anything else in all creation, will be able to separate us from the love of God in Christ Jesus our Lord.

Returning to the Letter to the Romans, we see that Paul makes it clear that our hope is in Christ, as he recounts the power of the Lord as demonstrated by the sacrifice he made on our behalf. We find hope beyond our immediate circumstances with the promise of his presence in our lives—and beyond. But if that fulfillment vision is not trusted and understood, then a different path lies before these young Christians. Having given the warnings and communicated the importance of staying connected as Christians, Paul continues with a non-humorous description of the dark pathway of the philosophy of fatalism and apathy, were it to become the chosen way to follow.

---

**People lose their way and turn to behavior that does not lead to truth/causes harm.**

---

> 4:18 *They are darkened in their understanding, alienated from the life of God because of their ignorance and hardness of heart.*

For his Ephesian readers, Paul traces results that come with a cynical discounting of meaning. He follows the futility word in his description of such a pathway, first with the word "darkened" (*skotos*). Shadows affect the way we see and understand the pathway itself. His next word is "alienation" (*apallotrio*), which means "being set loose in the loneliness of estrangement." This word is also used by Paul when he writes, "And you who were once estranged and hostile in mind, doing evil deeds" (Col 1:21). In this instance he pairs alienation with another even stronger estrangement word (*echthos*), the New Testament word for "enemy." The consequential thinking reveals the attitude, "If I can find someone to blame as an enemy, I can justify my estrangement."

Our Lord uses this extreme estrangement word and tells us what to do with those who are supposed enemies. The answer to this

## SECTION III: PAUL OFFERS ADVICE FOR THE PEOPLE OF THE GOSPEL

kind of behavior is found in the Sermon on the Mount. Remember that Jesus tells us how to relate to those we perceive as our enemies. "You have heard that it was said, 'You shall love your neighbor and hate your enemy.' But I say to you, 'Love your enemies and pray for those who persecute you so that you may be children of your father in heaven'" (Matt 5:43–45a). Jesus gives the better way.

The pathway of futility becomes even darker when Paul adds to his list one more lonely word, *porosis*, which means "hard." He describes the traveler on the way downward as having "hardness of heart," perhaps chosen as a protection from involvement with others. The word for "hard" is actually the Greek word for "petrify." In Mark's Gospel, an event in the ministry of Jesus shows how hardness reveals the lack of sensitivity that separates one from another.

### Mark 3:1–6

### *A Challenge to Hardness of Heart*

It made Jesus angry to see hardness of heart of one against another, especially against someone who was in need of care.

> Again, he entered the synagogue, and a man was there who had a withered hand. ² They watched him to see whether he would cure him on the Sabbath, so that they might accuse him. ³ And he said to the man who had the withered hand, "Come forward." ⁴ Then he said to them, "Is it lawful to do good or to do harm on the Sabbath, to save life or to kill?" But they were silent. ⁵ He looked around at them with anger; he was grieved at their hardness of heart and said to the man, "Stretch out your hand." He stretched it out, and his hand was restored. ⁶ The Pharisees went out and immediately conspired with the Herodians against him, how to destroy him.

The Lord was not preoccupied with whether he should heal or not heal on the Sabbath. He knew what was most important and what he needed to do in the face of such a show of hardness of heart. He knew what had to be done—and he did it! He healed the man. The reaction of those who saw this goodness was to plot against the man who was good, Jesus. The conspirators, emboldened by their rules, had lost sensitivity and empathy for the person who was suffering.

> 4:19 *They have lost all sensitivity and have abandoned themselves to licentiousness, greedy to practice every kind of impurity.*

There is one more isolating stopping place. The text says, "They have lost all *sensitivity*..." This is the word *apalogeo*, which describes a lack of ordinary human feelings, including empathy for the feelings of others around us. This angry pathway ironically can lead either to the choice of personal withdrawal into aloneness, or to moving in the opposite direction into reckless (even aggressive) behavior towards others.

The text continues with the results of that abandonment, a sentence made stark by the use of these words: "licentiousness, greedy to practice every kind of immorality." The word *aselgeia* is the strongest Greek word for intemperance in interpersonal behavior. Somehow, the darkness and hardness have become highly active. The people have made interpersonal behavior aggressively punitive and even violent. It has become the dark path of the hardness of heart.

## Ephesians 4:20–32

### A Word Game for Discipleship

> [20] That is not the way you learned Christ! [21] For surely you have heard about him and were taught in him, as truth is in Jesus. [22] You were taught to put away your former way of life, your old self, corrupt and deluded by its lusts, [23] and to be renewed in the spirit of your minds, [24] and to clothe yourselves with the new self, created according to the likeness of God in true righteousness and holiness.
>
> [25] So then, putting away falsehood, let all of us speak the truth to our neighbors, for we are members of one another. [26] Be angry but do not sin; do not let the sun go

## SECTION III: PAUL OFFERS ADVICE FOR THE PEOPLE OF THE GOSPEL

down on your anger, [27] and do not make room for the devil. [28] Thieves must give up stealing; rather let them labor and work honestly with their own hands, so as to have something to share with the needy. [29] Let no evil talk come out of your mouths, but only what is useful for building up, as there is need, so that your words may give grace to those who hear. [30] And do not grieve the Holy Spirit of God, with which you were marked with a seal for the day of redemption. [31] Put away from you all bitterness and wrath and anger and wrangling and slander, together with all malice, [32] and be kind to one another, tenderhearted, forgiving one another, as God in Christ has forgiven you.

Fortunately for both the Ephesians and for us who read the text in our century, our wise teacher and coach does not leave us in that despairing and dark pathway.

---

***Followers of Jesus Christ are called to be renewed and take on behaviors that reflect the Lord's teachings on how to live.***

---

4:20, 21 *That is not the way you learned Christ! For surely you have heard about him and were taught in him, as truth is in Jesus.*

In light of the concerns that occupy Paul's mind, he points the people back to Christ and Christ's way of teaching the truth. Upon that foundation, he sets up for them (and for us) an exercise of repentance and a caring, self-confessional, both a physical and emotional way to refocus the discipleship journey away from the bad path of unrighteousness toward the good journey of righteousness.

4:22–24 *You were taught to put away your former way of life, your old self, corrupt and deluded by its lusts, and to be renewed in the spirit of your minds, and to clothe yourselves with the new self, created according to the likeness of God in true righteousness and holiness.*

## PART 7: THE TRUTH OF THE GOSPEL IS THE AXIOM

At this point, Paul assures his friends at Ephesus of what is better: the way they learned from Christ. He lists the virtues and urges the followers to practice such behavior in their own lives.

> 4:25–32 *So then, putting away falsehood, let all of us speak the truth to our neighbors, for we are members of one another. Be angry but do not sin; do not let the sun go down on your anger, and do not make room for the devil. Thieves must give up stealing; rather let them labor and work honestly with their own hands, so as to have something to share with the needy. Let no evil talk come out of your mouths, but only what is useful for building up, as there is need, so that your words may give grace to those who hear. And do not grieve the Holy Spirit of God, with which you were marked with a seal for the day of redemption. Put away from you all bitterness and wrath and anger and wrangling and slander, together with all malice, and be kind to one another, tenderhearted, forgiving one another, as God in Christ has forgiven you.*

Paul sets up a dual set of repentance-and-resolve sentences that we now choose. I call this a word game. He gives it to these disciples to self-teach a way toward making right decisions here and now, and also as a way to repent: each begins with a strong verb of repentance. We are to "put away" our former way of living—"our old self" when we followed a wrong way—and now we are to clothe ourselves with the newness of righteousness. He lists these faithful discipleship "repentance and new resolve" pairs through the remaining writing in chapter 4.

It is a "put off" <—> "put on" game:

| | |
|---|---|
| Put off falsehoods | Put on the truth |
| Put off sin | Put on resolution to anger |
| Put off the devil | Put on protection offered through Christ |
| Put off stealing | Put on honest work |

SECTION III: PAUL OFFERS ADVICE FOR THE PEOPLE OF THE GOSPEL

| | |
|---|---|
| Put off evil talk | Put on words of grace |
| Put off grievances for the Holy Spirit | Put on the mark of redemption |
| Put off bitterness and wrath | Put on kindness, tender-heartedness, and forgiveness |

The whole exercise has unmissable marks of wit and even whimsy. Note that Paul includes members of the church who may still be thieves (perhaps dice players). One of the best pairs in this discipleship word game comes early, "*Be angry*, but *do not sin*—do not let the sun go down on your anger." If you do that, you make a place for the devil. This reminds us that our choices and our behaviors do have consequences. Note also that within this very specific paragraph of wise ethical counsel is the fascinating phrase, "do not grieve the Holy Spirit." It is clear that what grieves God's heart is our lack of practical, person-to-person caring and tenderheartedness that originates from the caring heart of God in Christ.

*Our behavior can lead to an opening for evil.*

Over and over Paul entreats his readers to put away their former way of life, deluded by excessive desires and fears, and to put on their new self, created in the likeness of God. As he continues his word game challenge, it is clear that his understanding of repentance is personal and concrete. In John Mackay's words:

> It is important to observe that the universal dualism here alluded to is not an absolute or an ultimate dualism. It is, however, a real dualism. It is not a duality constituted by a mere difference of viewpoint, such as the classical distinction between sensed interpretation of diverse or contradictory phenomena. There is in the universe a very real and grave conflict of spiritual forces . . .[2]

2. Mackay, *God's Order*, 26.

PART 7: THE TRUTH OF THE GOSPEL IS THE AXIOM

This whole discourse reminds me of one Christian leader who was a great mentor for me, especially during my years as a student at Princeton Theological Seminary, and then in my early years as pastor for university students at University Presbyterian Church, Seattle. She was lovingly and with great respect called "Teacher," and that she was: a warm-hearted and positive influence in my life. Miss Mears, as she was called, was an inspiration for many young pastors like me during her years as Director of Christian Education, including the College and Young Adult Ministry, at Hollywood Presbyterian Church in Hollywood, California, where she was known as Dr. Henrietta Mears.[3] I remember many of her teachings on the meaning of discipleship. In my memory is an unforgettable story she told of her trip to California as a young Bible teacher, to begin her ministry at the Hollywood Church.

Dr. Mears had lived in Minneapolis and was riding on the long passenger train trip to California. She told us of the regular clicking sound of the train's wheels on the steel tracks. And she reported that into her mind came the discipleship passage from Paul's letter to the Ephesians, chapter 4. She began to say to herself the words of Paul: "put away" wrangling, "put on" kindness, "put away" your old life, "put on" your new life in Christ. She may have even said "put off" thieving, "put on" honest work, and then be able to help the needy. She entertained those of us who were listening to the Bible study, but she also endeared to us Paul's words in our favor, because she also saw the wonderful humor and goodness of the gospel.

Because of that memory, I have treasured in a very personal way St. Paul's whimsical word games of repentance and resolve that give this important rhythm of "put off" <—> "put on" in Ephesians 4 and 5.

---

3. Henrietta Mears (1890–1963) was known as the innovative and dynamic Director of Christian Education at Hollywood Presbyterian Church. In her role as Christian educator, author, and evangelist, this "teacher," as she was called had a profound impact on evangelical Christianity in the twentieth century.

**SECTION III: PAUL OFFERS ADVICE FOR THE PEOPLE OF THE GOSPEL**

In the next pages, Paul reminds the readers to follow God as beloved children, and live in love because Christ loved us and gave himself for us.

## Part 8: **Walk in the Light**

### Ephesians 5:1-2

#### Copy and Follow Love

¹ Therefore be imitators of God, as beloved children, ² and live in love, as Christ loved us and gave himself up for us, a fragrant offering and sacrifice to God.

PAUL SETS FORTH A course to follow, which is to look to God to understand how to behave.

> 5:1 *Therefore be imitators of God, as beloved children . . .*

As followers of Jesus we are encouraged to imitate, copy, and test the truth of the gospel. It is almost a dare from the apostle to try on for size the love that God has shown us as children, and then to live in that love. God's grace deserves our copying. It is the gift revealed in the person of Jesus. *Memeomai*, "imitate," is not a primary source word; it is a secondary word of learning. It is a telling of truth, not of our own creation but of our discovery. What does God do in the circumstances, as shown through the life of Christ? In Greek, the word for "remember" draws linguistically from the same root word, *memeomai*, to become a part of the new word, *mimneskoua*. To "remember" means "to call to mind." This becomes a vital faith word, with twenty-three uses in the New Testament. Read how St. Peter explains why he baptized the Gentile, Cornelius: "I *remembered* the word of the Lord, how he had said, 'John baptized with water but you will be baptized with the Holy Spirit'" (Acts 11:16). Imitation is learning by observation, testing, and copying. In Ephesians 5:1-2, Paul is

SECTION III: PAUL OFFERS ADVICE FOR THE PEOPLE OF THE GOSPEL

reminding his Ephesian friends to remember their experiences of being loved by the Lord of life.

---

*Celebrate with joy the receiving and sharing of grace.*

---

We are to remember and to imitate what J. R. R. Tolkien describes as "the sudden turn of joy." Tolkien describes the joy of the eucatastrophic breakthrough of the grace of Christ, when God's love becomes ours to know, perhaps for the very first time. The author does this in *The Lord of the Rings*, a story of adventure that symbolizes the reality of the goodness of God's joyous grace. He offers more insight on the joy we discover in an essay he titled "On Fairy Stories."

> . . . this joy which is one of the things which fairy-stories can produce supremely well, is not essentially 'escapist, nor fugitive'. In its fairy-tale—or otherworld—setting, it is a sudden and miraculous grace: never to be counted on to recur. It does not deny the existence of dyscatastrophe, of sorrow and failure: the possibility of these is necessary to the joy of deliverance; it denies (in the face of much evidence, if you will) universal final defeat and in so far is evangelium, giving a fleeting glimpse of Joy, Joy beyond the walls of the world, poignant as grief.
>
> It is the mark of a good fairy-story, of the higher or more complete kind, that however wild its events, however fantastic or terrible the adventures, it can give to child or man that hears it, when the 'turn' comes, a catch of the breath, a beat and lifting of the heart.[1]

Writing to adult readers, Paul makes use of the oldest way of learning: children learn by copying, by imitating what new information or skill the mom, dad, or teacher wants them to know and make their own. In this text, Paul invites Ephesian believers—young or old, and even those who are not yet believers—to learn

---

1. Tolkien, "On Fairy Stories," 81.

the greatest of all truths, the love that finds us, the love that is in our behalf because of the sacrifice of Jesus.

Most of the uses of the word "imitate" in New Testament texts are presented as "teaching by doing" advice, an approach used by other writers as well. Paul encourages those who receive his letters to imitate his own personal discipleship, as he follows Jesus Christ. This theme is confirmed in other sources:

> "I appeal to you, then, be imitators of me" (1 Cor 4:16).
>
> "For you, brothers and sisters, became imitators of the churches of God in Christ Jesus . . . " (1 Thess 2:14).
>
> "For you yourselves know how you ought to imitate us . . . " (2 Thess 3:7).
>
> "Beloved do not imitate what is evil, but imitate what is good" (3 John 11).
>
> "Remember your leaders, those who spoke the word of God to you, consider the outcomes of their way of life and imitate their faith. Jesus Christ is the same yesterday and today and forever" (Heb 13:7, 8).

In each case, the strategy is clear. "To be an imitator" is a coaching word used by teachers.

> 5:2 . . . *and live in love, as Christ loved us and gave himself up for us, a fragrant offering and sacrifice to God.*

One resolution stands alone. Paul concludes the exercise in repentance with the healing words of forgiveness, "Live in love, as Christ loved us." God, in his son, Jesus Christ, has forgiven our sins. The list includes what we have called out as contrary to how we want to live, and who we want to be, as redeemed men and women.

SECTION III: PAUL OFFERS ADVICE FOR THE PEOPLE OF THE GOSPEL

## Ephesians 5:3–14

### A List for Practical Christianity

> ³ But fornication and impurity of any kind, or greed, must not even be mentioned among you, as is proper among saints. ⁴ Entirely out of place is obscene, silly, and vulgar talk; but instead, let there be thanksgiving. ⁵ Be sure of this, that no fornicator or impure person, or one who is greedy (that is, an idolater), has any inheritance in the kingdom of Christ and of God.
>
> ⁶ Let no one deceive you with empty words, for because of these things the wrath of God comes on those who are disobedient. ⁷ Therefore do not be associated with them. ⁸ For once you were darkness, but now in the Lord you are light. Live as children of light— ⁹ for the fruit of the light is found in all that is good and right and true. ¹⁰ Try to find out what is pleasing to the Lord. ¹¹ Take no part in the unfruitful works of darkness, but instead expose them. ¹² For it is shameful even to mention what such people do secretly; ¹³ but everything exposed by the light becomes visible, ¹⁴ for everything that becomes visible is light. Therefore it says, "Sleeper, awake! Rise from the dead, and Christ will shine on you."

In the interpersonal ethical counsel in this chapter, Paul combines three kinds of behavior to avoid.

> 5:3–5 *But fornication and impurity of any kind, or greed, must not even be mentioned among you, as is proper among saints. Entirely out of place is obscene, silly, and vulgar talk; but instead, let there be thanksgiving. Be sure of this, that no fornicator or impure person, or one who is greedy (that is, an idolater), has any inheritance in the kingdom of Christ and of God.*

Paul continues with the "put off" <—> "put on" word game:

## PART 8: WALK IN THE LIGHT

| | |
|---|---|
| Put off behaviors of impurity of any kind | Put on behavior that avoids such impurities |
| Put off talk of obscenities | Put on words of thanksgiving |
| Put off idolatry | Put on that which honors our inheritance |

The writer warns first against sexual immorality, *porneo*, in a generalized definition as lewdness. The second word is *akatharsa*, the word for uncleanness. The third word is *pleonektes*, usually translated "greed." Notice that he combines immoral interpersonal behavior with the word "greed," which describes obsessive desire to have what is not rightly my own. This advice correlates with the tenth commandment in the Mosaic Covenant of the Law, "You shall not covet your neighbor's house; you shall not covet your neighbor's wife, male or female slave, or ox, or donkey, or anything that belongs to your neighbor" (Exod 20:17). Paul warns that such behavior is not proper among saints. The distortions of lewdness or greediness do not harmonize with our inheritance in the kingdom of God. He even cautions against conversations about these behaviors.

The apostle Paul's word game illustrates a practical way to repent of the darkness and to see clearly in the light. Put off the dark ways, and put on the new self that seeks to imitate the grace of Christ, who is the Lord of light and love. We now can enjoy the freedom that lives out redeeming forgiveness and enables us to decide in favor of goodness. Our conversation should focus on that truth. Shun destructive conversation, especially gossip, in the community of faith. He calls such conversation "obscene, silly and vulgar."

I believe that Paul advises Christians to avoid such subject matter as a preoccupation even in judgmental conversation about wrongdoers, because we are then tempted to rejoice in the downfall of sinners, rather than in their rescue from harm. It would be unwise for the saints at Ephesus to drift toward either the wrongness of self-righteousness or the wrongness of sin. He reminds them that these behaviors, the first two in this list, are immoral interpersonal offenses, while the third, greed, is the offense of idolatry.

The word he uses here for "idolatry" is the Greek *eidolon*, understood as "image, shadow, phantom." In the New Testament, the Greek term literally is "idol." Paul's earliest book in the New Testament is 1 Thessalonians, and his first use of the word is interesting because of the way he describes it. Paul reports on the healthy faith of the Thessalonian Christians. He remarks that their faith is encouraging to other new Christians in the Roman province of Macedonia and as far away as Corinth. He writes, "For the word of the Lord has sounded forth from you in every place. Your faith in God has become known . . . how you turned to God from idols, to serve a living and true God . . ." (1 Thess 1:8–9). In other words, they trusted in the living God who makes himself known to us, not in a shadow or image or phantom. This understanding of what constitutes an idol is clear in all uses of this word in the New Testament.

> 5:6–9 *Let no one deceive you with empty words, for because of these things the wrath of God comes on those who are disobedient. Therefore do not be associated with them. For once you were darkness, but now in the Lord you are light. Live as children of light—for the fruit of the light is found in all that is good and right and true.*

Put off the deception of empty words, or else we may find ourselves focused on what is empty and emptying, Paul continues, with a repeat of the warning that comes with deceit—the use of the word *planeo* discussed in the previous chapter of Ephesians. We are advised not to delight in judgmental conversation that becomes attentive to and fascinated by wrongdoers and what they do. Instead, Paul says to "put on the light."

---

*As believers in Christ, we are
no longer to live in darkness.*

---

## PART 8: WALK IN THE LIGHT

> 5:10–14 *Try to find out what is pleasing to the Lord. Take no part in the unfruitful works of darkness, but instead expose them. For it is shameful even to mention what such people do secretly; but everything exposed by the light becomes visible, for everything that becomes visible is light. Therefore it says, "Sleeper, awake! Rise from the dead, and Christ will shine on you."*

Paul tells us, instead, to focus our eyes, minds, and hearts on the goodness and truth of light, not the various shadows of darkness.

There is more to think about in the "put off" <—> "put on" word game:

| | |
|---|---|
| Put off what is unfruitful | Put on what exposes darkness and is pleasing |
| Put off gossip | Put on that which enlightens for the good |

As young believers we should keep our eyes on the good, the true, and the righteous character of the Lord of light. The secrets of the darkness do not deserve center stage.

At this point, Paul also quotes a first-century baptismal hymn found only here in the Bible as the better pathway: "Sleeper, awake! Rise from the dead, and Christ will shine on you."

## Ephesians 5:15–20

### Guidance for How to Live

> [15] Be careful then how you live, not as unwise people but as wise, [16] making the most of the time, because the days are evil. [17] So do not be foolish, but understand what the will of the Lord is. [18] Do not get drunk with wine, for that is debauchery; but be filled with the Spirit, [19] as you sing psalms and hymns and spiritual songs among yourselves,

> singing and making melody to the Lord in your hearts, [20] giving thanks to God the Father at all times and for everything in the name of our Lord Jesus Christ.

Paul continues to assure his friends at Ephesus of what is the better way: the way they learned from Christ. As he points to the right pathway for our life journey, we are told to freely make choices as disciples of Jesus Christ, choosing words that are a permanent part of the *axios* teaching theme of Paul as trainer and life coach for the young Christians at Ephesus.

---

*To live in the light requires awareness and intentional behavior.*

---

> 5:15–18b *Be careful then how you live, not as unwise people but as wise, making the most of the time, because the days are evil. So do not be foolish, but understand what the will of the Lord is. Do not get drunk with wine, for that is debauchery; but be filled with the Spirit . . .*

And Paul continues to add to the "put off" <—> "put on" word game:

| | |
|---|---|
| Put off yielding to time that embraces evil | Put on wisdom in your use of time |
| Put off being foolish | Put on that which recognizes the will of the Lord |
| Put off debauchery | Put on singing and melodies in your heart |

Paul now gives advice about wisdom as a virtue: be careful to live not as unwise, but as wise. Paul is writing in the company of Solomon's wisdom books, Ecclesiastes and Proverbs. He urges a careful use of time.

## PART 8: WALK IN THE LIGHT

We are not certain what Paul intends by the phrase "because the days are evil." *Poneros*, "the objective evil," is the word for *evil* that is used. We ask, "Is he repeating his own statement from the Galatian letter that he wrote near the beginning of his teaching ministry? "Grace to you and peace from God our Father and the Lord Jesus Christ, who gave himself for our sins to set us free from the present evil age . . ." (Gal 1:4). We will see him use this same word later in the discussion on the subject of evil in Ephesians 6, "our struggle is against . . . the spiritual forces of *evil* in the heavenly places."

> 5:18(b)–20 . . . *but be filled with the Spirit, as you sing psalms and hymns and spiritual songs among yourselves, singing and making melody to the Lord in your hearts, giving thanks to God the Father at all times, and for everything in the name of our Lord Jesus Christ.*

Note that in these verses that Paul breaks from warnings and shifts to singing and preparing for the outpouring of joy to be found in the relationship with the Lord that grounds all of our relationships with one another. Consistent with the letters of this apostle, he returns always to remind the reader to give thanks for everything that the Lord gives us in our lives.

The text will then move forward to focus on a particular relationship, that between wife and husband.

## Ephesians 5:21–33

### Find Your Station in Reverence to Christ

> [21] Be subject to one another out of reverence for Christ.
>
> [22] Wives, be subject to your husbands as you are to the Lord. [23] For the husband is the head of the wife just as Christ is the head of the church, the body of which he is the Savior. [24] Just as the church is subject to Christ, so also wives ought to be, in everything, to their husbands.

## SECTION III: PAUL OFFERS ADVICE FOR THE PEOPLE OF THE GOSPEL

<sup>25</sup> Husbands, love your wives, just as Christ loved the church and gave himself up for her, <sup>26</sup> in order to make her holy by cleansing her with the washing of water by the word, <sup>27</sup> so as to present the church to himself in splendor, without a spot or wrinkle or anything of the kind—yes, so that she may be holy and without blemish. <sup>28</sup> In the same way, husbands should love their wives as they do their own bodies. He who loves his wife loves himself. <sup>29</sup> For no one ever hates his own body, but he nourishes and tenderly cares for it, just as Christ does for the church, <sup>30</sup> because we are members of his body. <sup>31</sup> "For this reason a man will leave his father and mother and be joined to his wife, and the two will become one flesh." <sup>32</sup> This is a great mystery, and I am applying it to Christ and the church. <sup>33</sup> Each of you, however, should love his wife as himself, and a wife should respect her husband.

The words are often mistaken to imply authority one over the other. But this is not my interpretation. The advice does not imply subjugation but sets the relationship between husband and wife on the premise that all relationships are built upon the Lord as the foundation. Paul sees this relationship as one that is to be filled with singing and thankfulness.

> 5:21-23 *Be subject to one another out of reverence for Christ. Wives, be subject to your husbands as you are to the Lord. For the husband is the head of the wife just as Christ is the head of the church, the body of which he is the Savior.*

We examine these verses first by understanding the key word in this section—"reverence," which is placed at the end of the opening sentence. Here, the word *phobeo* is used for reverence toward God. It is a word that connotes "fear, astonishment, amazement." Located forty-seven times in the New Testament, this expression of fear is not "terror" but an expression filled with joy. My favorite use of *phobeo* is in the text that tells of the women who first discovered the resurrection of Jesus. "So they left the tomb quickly with fear and great joy, and ran to tell his disciples" (Matt 28:8). The relationship between husband and wife is set, then, upon this foundation of an amazement that draws from their relationship with Christ.

Discussion of the interaction between wives and husbands is predicated upon the awesome nature of this joy. In the next section we will go back and fill in the idea of "making melody to the Lord" as previously stated by explaining that marriage is built upon the notion that it is a place, "tasso," that draws forth singing and prepares us for one of the most joyous and dramatic stations of our lives, which by God's grace will endure through years of life together with anniversaries, children, extended families, and even grandchildren.

---

*In marriage, husband and wife are stationed in a mutual relationship described as existing out of honor for the Lord and at a post beholden to the Lord.*

---

Now we can return to the first part of the sentence, "Be subject." The word "subject" in Greek is *tasso*, and it refers to a post or a stationing that carries the mandate that we have obligations to one another because of Christ. One example of this word *tasso* is found in Acts 15, when the first-century church council was held in Jerusalem to decide whether Greek believers required the covenant sign of circumcision. The text tells us that Barnabas and Paul were designated to be present at that meeting: "Paul and Barnabas and some others were *appointed*." The word *tasso* is used to explain why they were present. It was their post, and they were obligated to be there for a purpose. This word *tasso* in Greek carries with it the idea "to make precise arrangement" or "assign to a post or station."

Paul tells of this discipleship posting, and that we welcome this mandate in our life, because of our reverence for Christ. The base word can also be understood according to the episode when Priscilla and Aquila were ordered by the Emperor Claudius, along with other Jews, to leave Rome (Acts 18:2). Here the word is *diatasso*—"stationed away, ordered." They were mandated to be away from Rome. This explanation sets us up to understand that

## SECTION III: PAUL OFFERS ADVICE FOR THE PEOPLE OF THE GOSPEL

as Christians, we all have a posting mandate toward one another because of Jesus.

---

*The concept of "be subject" connotes a relationship that constitutes a post—and is not to be confused with subjugation.*

---

This word *tasso* is interwoven into Paul's pastoral teaching concerning our discipleship obligations to each other. The opening words of this text, "Be subject," are edifying for both wife and husband. Paul makes use of *upotasso* in his pastoral discussion of marriage as one of the main postings for a man, or a woman, who falls in love and gets married, and the joy of family that results. The words "Be subject" are then interwoven in the text. In Greek the word "subject" is *upotasso*, which combines the word *tasso* with the word *upo*, which means "under." Translated, the word becomes "submit to, become subject to," as a soldier or diplomat is stationed to a city or country. The mandate of love, respect, and faithful caring is established as the Lord's gift to us, as in the total *axios* teaching we have focused on in chapters 4 and 5. "Therefore as beloved children, we live in love, as Christ loved us and gave himself up for us, a fragrant offering and sacrifice to God" (Eph 5:1–2).

Recognizing that the mystery in marriage is more than just the love between a man and woman who love each other, the posting together also becomes history-making. Therefore, a wife and husband are placed in a station of responsibility. Dietrich Bonhoeffer further explains this insight in a chapter titled, "A Wedding Sermon from a Prison Cell, May 1943."

> In your love you see only the heaven of your own happiness but in marriage you are placed in a post of responsibility towards the world and mankind. Your love is your own private possession, but marriage is more than something personal—it is a status, an office. Just as it is the crown, not just the will to rule, that makes the king,

## PART 8: WALK IN THE LIGHT

so it is marriage, and not merely your love for each other, that joins you together in the sight of God and man.[2]

Now St. Paul makes use of this stationing word for our responsible discipleship in the ancient human institution of marriage. The teaching to the Christians at Ephesus begins with both the man and the woman who intend marriage or have married; *upotasso* acknowledges the mutual and joyous stationing in this relationship. Therefore, when we make the commitment we both have chosen, in asking each other to share life together, we freely welcome being stationed together. Paul is defining marriage as a station we submit to: first to each other, and then held together under the post of responsibility that carries obligations in reverence to the Lord of life. The *upotasso* is because of his grace first of all, which explains the joyous beginning of this whole text.

Second to the mystery of "Christ and his church" is this sense of amazement, the joy of this post.

> 5:25–30 *Husbands, love your wives, just as Christ loved the church and gave himself up for her, in order to make her holy by cleansing her with the washing of water by the word, so as to present the church to himself in splendor, without a spot or wrinkle or anything of the kind—yes, so that she may be holy and without blemish. In the same way, husbands should love their wives as they do their own bodies. He who loves his wife loves himself. For no one ever hates his own body, but he nourishes and tenderly cares for it, just as Christ does for the church, because we are members of his body.*

---

**In marriage, the commitment to each other has significance beyond the husband and wife.**

---

The importance of this "station" is that it "stations" both husband and wife to a post in history, and to the future generations of which we will be a part. Marriage is part of a greater dimension

2. Bonhoeffer, *Letters and Papers from Prison*, 43.

## SECTION III: PAUL OFFERS ADVICE FOR THE PEOPLE OF THE GOSPEL

that Paul explains: "This is a great mystery, and I am applying it to Christ and the church."

Notice the equality in marriage that is announced at the beginning. Then in the final sentence of his teaching on marriage, he makes the equality of station very clear. My sense of the text's translation is that love and respect one to another is fundamental.

> 5:31-33 *"For this reason a man will leave his father and mother and be joined to his wife, and the two will become one flesh." This is a great mystery, and I am applying it to Christ and the church. Each of you, however, should love his wife as himself, and a wife should respect her husband.*

This is the start of a brand new relationship, with the young adults making their own decision to marry. Paul quotes from the Old Testament to describe the decision we make in the action and commitment to each other—husband to wife, and wife to husband (see Gen 2:4). Paul is celebrating this station and makes clear that this relationship is one of equality and shared joy.

# Part 9: **Stand with Strength**

### Ephesians 6:1-9

### The Mediator of Relationships

Children, obey your parents in the Lord, for this is right. ² "Honor your father and mother"—this is the first commandment with a promise: ³ "so that it may be well with you and you may live long on the earth."

⁴ And, fathers, do not provoke your children to anger, but bring them up in the discipline and instruction of the Lord.

⁵ Slaves, obey your earthly masters with fear and trembling, in singleness of heart, as you obey Christ; ⁶ not only while being watched, and in order to please them, but as slaves of Christ, doing the will of God from the heart. ⁷ Render service with enthusiasm, as to the Lord and not to men and women, ⁸ knowing that whatever good we do, we will receive the same again from the Lord, whether we are slaves or free.

⁹ And, masters, do the same to them. Stop threatening them, for you know that both of you have the same Master in heaven, and with him there is no partiality.

"CHILDREN, OBEY YOUR PARENTS in the Lord . . ." Notice, first of all, that in this family text, the "in the Lord" clause is vital to the meaning of the whole sentence. Jesus stands in between parents and children, children and parents. Paul's description of the human-to-human relationships that we experience through

## SECTION III: PAUL OFFERS ADVICE FOR THE PEOPLE OF THE GOSPEL

our lifetimes helps us understand this good and liberating truth of the gospel of Jesus.

> 6:1-4 *Children, obey your parents in the Lord, for this is right. "Honor your father and mother"—this is the first commandment with a promise: "so that it may be well with you and you may live long on the earth." And, fathers, do not provoke your children to anger, but bring them up in the discipline and instruction of the Lord.*

It is Jesus who is the mediator. He protects both myself as a person and other persons too with his Lordship and grace. Even in a family this is true. Again quoting the young German pastor Dietrich Bonhoeffer, we observe that he saw this foundation clearly. In his reflections on the "in the Lord" phrase, Bonhoeffer argues that as humans we do not have direct interpersonal relationships; rather, we have mediated relationships. "This is the meaning of the proposition that we can meet others only through the mediation of Christ."[1] This sentence clearly states that as a Christian, I know two things about every person I meet. First, I know that that person is a sinner like I am, which is some protection against disappointment when people let us down. Second, I also know something even better, and it is that this person—whoever he or she is—is a person beloved. I learned this from Christ, who is the mediator between us. Even if that other person I meet does not know it, I know it. This is the truth, the *axios*. With this basic truth in mind, Bonhoeffer was able to write, "Spiritual love does not desire but rather serves, it loves an enemy as a brother, it originates neither in the brother nor in the enemy but in Christ and his word."[2]

We are grateful to Bonhoeffer, and to St. Paul, for this protection against child abuse or parental abuse. We can claim the protective love and goodness and even humor that comes from that double knowing: that Jesus Christ is in between, as the mediator for each person in a family—or, as we see later, even in a workplace.

---

1. Bonhoeffer, *Life Together*, 86.
2. Bonhoeffer, *Life Together*, 35.

PART 9: STAND WITH STRENGTH

*The concept for "obey" is grounded in the act of listening.*

Now the word "obey" in our Ephesian text needs to be rightly understood. The word used extensively in the Bible is *upakuo*, literally interpreted as "give ear to, listen." I believe that this precise meaning is more helpful for an understanding of Paul's intention than the word "obey," which lacks the helpful overtones that are present in the word "listen." In the letter to the people at Philippi Paul explains the full identification of Jesus with each of us (Phil 2:6–11). Then he says "As you have always listened [*upakuo*] to me . . ." (Phil 2:12). In my view, the word "obey" used here in the NRSV text is not in keeping with the tone of Paul's writing.

For me, "listen" is certainly the right word. It is the best obedience word, too, because of its significant use in the Old Testament. Deuteronomy begins the recital of the Ten Commandments with the Hebrew word *shemah*, "*Hear* O Israel." The best thing about this respectful word is that it invites negotiation from the hearer, as well as the speaker. The importance of "listen" and "hear" is vital for father/daughter/son or mother/daughter/son negotiation. It also harmonizes best with intelligent discipline by older persons. To listen gives opportunity for interdependence built upon respect for one another's voice, particularly when you want to encourage a young person to gain independent executive brain development and moral self-responsibility, which will be required for individual decision-making and goal setting. When youth are able to listen, they gain from the wisdom of the older generations, and this helps them to make their own decisions. At the same time, when the position of the person sharing the wisdom is set within the parameters of freedom, it honors the voice of the child and can be character-building. When a child is expected to always conform to parental wishes simply to keep peace, the child does not necessarily integrate the learning into development that fosters strength—strength to withstand pressure, so that he or she can make good decisions in the face of external influences that could bring potential harm.

SECTION III: PAUL OFFERS ADVICE FOR THE PEOPLE OF THE GOSPEL

---

*The relationship of child to parent holds the qualities of honor and respect (and it is important that parents know they must earn this place through their actions, too).*

---

The call to children to actually hear what a parent is trying to say is then followed by the great word from the Ten Commandments: "Honor" (*timao*) your father and mother. Here the message is clear. Honor means to "estimate in worth." I like the Old Testament sense of the word *timao* as "weigh heavy," which carries respect for experience and also personal value. Paul notes the promise of reward for those who "weigh heavy" their parents. This rendering of the commandment supports the outcome: "Honor your father and your mother, as the Lord commanded you, so that your days may be long and that it may go well with you in the land that the Lord your God is giving you" (Deut 5:16).

Paul follows this counsel with words to fathers: "do not provoke." This is the word *paraorgizo*, which cautions the fathers to avoid an argument that ends badly (without resolution) so that the sun does go down on anger. The word in classical Greek is sometimes used physically to describe a fever at its highest point or "paroxysm." Paul here points out to fathers the grave consequences that can result from a provocation style that focuses on punishment rather than "discipline." Paul warns against provoking a son or daughter with such fierceness of rebuke that there is no way through the argument and it thereby becomes a pathway into alienation. He calls out to fathers to use the style of a teacher, *paideia*, to "be encouraging." This is the most common word in the New Testament for "teacher." In the first century, a teacher was always seen as an honored encourager. Paul's letter to Timothy gives us an example: "And the Lord's servant must not be quarrelsome but kindly to everyone, an apt teacher, patient, correcting opponents with gentleness" (2 Tim 2:24–25).

> 6:5–9 *Slaves, obey your earthly masters with fear and trembling, in singleness of heart, as you obey Christ; not*

## PART 9: STAND WITH STRENGTH

*only while being watched, and in order to please them, but as slaves of Christ, doing the will of God from the heart. Render service with enthusiasm, as to the Lord and not to men and women, knowing that whatever good we do, we will receive the same again from the Lord, whether we are slaves or free. And, masters, do the same to them. Stop threatening them, for you know that both of you have the same Master in heaven, and with him there is no partiality.*

Paul now gives pastoral advice to Christians who either are slaves in the Roman Empire or are slave owners. He uses the identical word that he gave to the sons and daughters for a family at Ephesus—"hear" your earthly master—but he makes their hearing a secondary mandate for the Christian slave, who has his ears mainly focused on the Lord Jesus Christ and his teaching. Therefore, in the sentence, the listening (*upakuo*) that previously regarded children now starts the sentence for the Christian slave, and that the strong "listen" verb governs his whole task. Not only is he or she to hear the master, but from the heart to hear Christ— and do the will of God, also from the heart, whether as a slave or free. The slave needs to listen to two masters, his employer and the Lord. This principle of double listening for a servant is also preserved in military codes of conduct that instruct an officer of lower rank to resist and not obey an illegal command given by an officer, even one of superior rank. The military code puts the person under the bigger value—under the law.

The next sentence is still governed by the word "listen/hear" but is now assigned to the owner of slaves. Paul starts the sentence about owners with this key word, writing, "The same do to them." Now it is clear that the owner must "listen" too. Paul reminds the Christian owner "for you know that both of you have the same master in heaven, and with him there is no partiality." The word here for "partiality" is *prosopolempsia*. It also appears in other places in the New Testament, e.g., "For God shows no partiality" (Rom 2:11). A different use of the word found in this citation gives caution, "My brothers and sisters, do you with your acts of *favoritism* really believe in our glorious Lord Jesus Christ?" (Jas

2:1). For Paul and James, the ground is level without discrimination. Here is more evidence of the authority of goodness for each of us to remember. The rule becomes to listen with double listening, two-way listening.

---

*Treating others as valued is the foremost aspect of positive relationships.*

---

## Ephesians 6:10–20

### Put on the Whole Armor

[10] Finally, be strong in the Lord and in the strength of his power. [11] Put on the whole armor of God, so that you may be able to stand against the wiles of the devil. [12] For our struggle is not against enemies of blood and flesh, but against the rulers, against the authorities, against the cosmic powers of this present darkness, against the spiritual forces of evil in the heavenly places. [13] Therefore take up the whole armor of God, so that you may be able to withstand on that evil day, and having done everything, to stand firm. [14] Stand therefore, and fasten the belt of truth around your waist, and put on the breastplate of righteousness. [15] As shoes for your feet put on whatever will make you ready to proclaim the gospel of peace. [16] With all of these, take the shield of faith, with which you will be able to quench all the flaming arrows of the evil one. [17] Take the helmet of salvation, and the sword of the Spirit, which is the word of God.

[18] Pray in the Spirit at all times in every prayer and supplication. To that end keep alert and always persevere in supplication for all the saints. [19] Pray also for me, so that when I speak, a message may be given to me to make known with boldness the mystery of the gospel, [20] for which I am an ambassador in chains. Pray that I may declare it boldly, as I must speak.

## PART 9: STAND WITH STRENGTH

This text from St. Paul will feature two key words in a dramatic way. Then, the apostle will create a parable that has become an unforgettable feature in this concluding chapter of Paul's Ephesian letter.

> 6:10–12 *Finally, be strong in the Lord and in the strength of his power. Put on the whole armor of God, so that you may be able to stand against the wiles of the devil. For our struggle is not against enemies of blood and flesh, but against the rulers, against the authorities, against the cosmic powers of this present darkness, against the spiritual forces of evil in the heavenly places.*

After praying for the people and giving advice on how to live in the world where they find themselves, Paul gives ways to thrive in living as a Christian in the midst of challenge and responsibility, including "be strong in the Lord." Watch for two key words. First, *endynamia*, "strength," which he commends to those young first-century Christians. The second keyword is *histemi*, "stand," a word that signifies stature. This word for "stand" has 154 uses in the New Testament.

The strength language comes first. Paul makes use of the word *endynamia*, from which we get the English word "dynamic." It means "power" and is used extensively in the New Testament. Here Paul adapts the root word for "power" with the use of a prefix, *en*, that shows it is "for us." The prefix *en-* means nearness, and it designates a close connection of this word for "strength" with the Lord. In his other writings, Paul uses this adapted word in his giving of assurance, "The Lord *strengthened* me" (2 Tim 4:17) and also, "as the Lord *strengthens* me" (Phil 4:13). This word denotes being empowered by the Lord. In this use of *endymania*, Paul makes it clear that the strength is not seen as power in itself but is connected to the Lord. He recognizes that power isolated from a healthy source can easily become cultic and tyrannical. "Might makes right" is always idolatry.

Paul makes use of two other power words that also gain their validity and healthy goodness from their source and purpose. Notice how they are combined with *endymania*. "Finally grow strong (*endymania*) in the Lord and in the strength (*kratos*) of his power."

*Kratos* is usually translated in the English text as "great," related to God's sovereign reign. This word points to the reigning authority of God. The last word in this sentence, *ischuo*, is also a word for "power," usually translated as "might" but here as "power" because of the sovereignty of God. With this threefold use of power language, each word dependent on the Lord as the source, Paul is assuring the young Christians at Ephesus of the source of strength that is theirs to claim. It comes from the Lord.

---

**Power is defined by the ability to stand at the post in which strength is derived from the Lord's authority.**

---

This teacher uses one more important discipleship word to prepare the young believers of Ephesus. It is the word "stand," *histemi*. "Put on the whole armor of God so that you may be able to stand." Paul has more to say about the extent of this word, "stand."

An interesting development occurred in the use of the Greek word "stand," *histemi*, through its use in Latin and English and its role in medical vocabulary. A medicine to relieve the runny nose or swollen eyes of an allergic reaction was called an "antihistamine" drug, since it relieves the physical discomfort of what feels like an attack on the body. The simple Greek word *histemi* "to stand," if it faces its opposite, becomes *antihistemi*, which means to withstand and oppose someone. We find the concept of *antihistemi*, where it is used to "withstand" dangerous winds, to "stand your ground," just as using antihistamine medication means to stand against the allergy invasion. That same *antihistemi* is used in Ephesians, not against an allergic reaction or a human enemy, but against the devil and spiritual rulers of darkness in heavenly realms of that evil day.

The apostle recognizes the evil day as the battle against cosmic evil, and he describes this battle as the main battle. It requires Christians to be strengthened in order to hold their ground when evil spiritual will battles against the goodness and will of God. This is the devil, who is described in the New Testament as the

## PART 9: STAND WITH STRENGTH

"evil one," *tou ponerou* (Matt 6:13). This word is also used to describe the devil in the Lord's Prayer, "but deliver us from the *evil one*." In this instance, the reference is *tou ponero*, which extends the meaning to "personal evil."

Evil is portrayed as temptation from spiritual darkness (heavenly places)—as in the New Testament references to angels who are in the darkness and oppose the truth of God, and people too. The angels of darkness are not named in the New Testament, except that the servants of the dragon oppose the good angel Michael in Revelation 12, where the angel Michael wins that great battle against the devil and his angels.

Paul makes clear that there are temptations to avoid, and that spiritual evil presents itself in the face of the journey to be disciples of the living Lord. He will now pick up on the theme of evil that he has referred to earlier. In so doing, he prepares us for an extensive discussion on the subject of evil as he moves forward to discuss the evil one—spiritual evil.

In four different places, Paul points in this letter to the existence of moral, personal will against the will of God in the spiritual realm of creation: the devil.

1. Paul makes two indirect references to this spiritual opponent. In Ephesians 1:20, he tells of the reign of Christ at the right hand of the Father. He follows that praise with these words: "Jesus Christ is far above all rule and authority and power and dominion and above every name that is named ... all things are under his feet..." (Eph 1:21–22).

2. Then Paul tells of the dangers to believers who, because of our sins, are "following the course of this world, following the ruler of the power of the air, the spirit that is now at work among those who are disobedient" (Eph 2:2).

3. Paul continues with a direct reference: "Do not let the sun go down on your anger, and do not make room for the devil" (Eph 4:26, 27).

4. A final reference to the devil is cited in the Ephesian letter: "Put on the whole armor of God, so that you may be able

## SECTION III: PAUL OFFERS ADVICE FOR THE PEOPLE OF THE GOSPEL

to stand against the wiles [the word is literally 'methods'] of the devil, for our struggle is not against enemies of flesh and blood but against the rulers . . . the cosmic powers of the present darkness, against spiritual forces of evil in the heavenly places" (Eph 6:11, 12).

From each of these statements by the apostle Paul, we see that this spiritual and moral will against the Lordship and goodness of God is the source of temptation to brothers and sisters of faith. In each reference, Paul does not minimize the power evil has to tempt by the "methods" of the evil one; temptation is his power. Still, he does not have any final power over anyone, because every man or woman's story is unfinished: we are all mid-story. Only Jesus Christ has the last word (Rom 8:31–34).

C. S. Lewis has a lively interchange in *The Screwtape Letters*, first published in 1941. It is a book of imaginary letters written by a senior tempter, Screwtape, to a junior tempter, Wormwood, who is in training and assigned to a young Englishman during World War II. This book has had a widespread influence on readers within the Christian faith and the world at large. The richness of Lewis's writing highlights the temptations that befall man.

Some years ago, I had the privilege of being invited to speak to a graduate student literature class at Peking University in Beijing, China. It turned out to be a very interesting one-day seminar. The subject to be discussed was *The Screwtape Letters*, which had been translated into Mandarin in China. The publisher there had retitled the book as *Letters From Hell*. The afternoon discussion became lively, with the character of Wormwood offering a key breakthrough moment. While reading together from the English text, a student asked me about the opening sentences of chapter 25 as cited below, and he asked me to explain the meaning of the word, "mere." In reading this book, remember to reverse what the senior devil, Screwtape, says to a junior devil:

> My dear Wormwood,
>
> The real trouble about the set your patient is living in is that it is *merely* Christian. They all have individual

interests, of course, but the bond remains mere Christianity. What we want, if men become Christians at all, is to keep them in the state of mind I call "Christianity And". You know—Christianity and the Crisis, Christianity and the New Psychology, Christianity and the New Order, Christianity and Faith Healing, Christianity and Psychical Research, Christianity and Vegetarianism, Christianity and Spelling Reform. If they must be Christians let them at least be Christians with a difference. Substitute for the faith itself some Fashion with a Christian colouring.[3]

The words, "*merely* Christian" and "mere Christianity" fascinated the young student. He asked, "Does Lewis mean 'bad Christianity, weak Christianity, small Christianity?'" He wondered how best to translate into Mandarin the concepts of "merely" and "mere." I thought to myself, "How best can I translate this, even into Shakespearean English?" The interchange provided a time for extensive and humorous discussion with all the students. Lewis makes use of the tempter, Screwtape, to point out the dangers of focusing on themes rather than on the person of Jesus. In so doing with wit and humor, Lewis uses satire to do the opposite and make the centrality of Christ accessible. Lewis's words "merely" and "mere" point to *basic* Christianity.

Years later, in 1960, Lewis decided as a Christian lay writer to add a second introduction to the 1941 edition, addressing a question he was often asked after the original publication of *The Screwtape Letters*: "Do you believe in the devil?" I suspected that some of the students in my seminar had similar questions. I am very much in agreement with his thoughtful literary and Christian reflections, including his response to that common question:

> Now, if by "the Devil" you mean a power opposite to God and, like God, self-existent from all eternity, the answer is certainly No. There is no uncreated being except God. God has no opposite. No being could attain a "perfect badness" opposite to the perfect goodness of God; for when you have taken away every kind of good thing

---

3. Lewis, *Screwtape Letters*, 91.

## SECTION III: PAUL OFFERS ADVICE FOR THE PEOPLE OF THE GOSPEL

(intelligence, will, memory, energy, and existence itself) there would be none of him left.

The proper question is whether I believe in devils. I do. That is to say, I believe in angels, and I believe that some of these, by the abuse of their free will, have become enemies to God and, as a corollary, to us. These we may call devils. They do not differ in nature from good angels, but their nature is depraved. Devil is the opposite of angel only as Bad Man is the opposite of Good Man. Satan, the leader or dictator of devils, is the opposite, not of God, but of Michael.

I believe this not in the sense that it is part of my creed, but in the sense that it is one of my opinions. My religion would not be in ruins if this opinion were shown to be false. Till that happens—and proofs of a negative are hard to come by—I shall retain it. It seems to me to explain a good many facts. It agrees with the plain sense of Scripture, the tradition of Christendom, and the beliefs of most men at most times. And it conflicts with nothing that any of the sciences has shown to be true.[4]

Paul calls for wisdom for all Christians who live, work, raise their families and share their faith in Christ in these less-than-ideal days. We must live wisely in the face of every kind of temptation. The source may be the evil one, but temptation also comes from our own desires, our fears, our ambitions, our anger or the anger of others, or the ambitious goals of others that seem to offer tempting success. In the book of Ephesians, we are told to beware of choosing bad behavior. Instead, in such a time Paul urges us to be filled with God's spirit. He is not pessimistic. We can resist temptation. We even are able to self-restrain our daily routines of living—for example, meeting the threat of potentially dangerous exposures to the coronavirus that has caused the present worldwide crisis. We should remember to sing out with heartfelt joy when we can and to give thanks to God for that which is good. As I write this commentary in Seattle, Washington, our country and the whole world is suffering from this deadly pandemic. Many

---

4. Lewis, *Screwtape Letters*, 6.

have been tempted to ignore the counsel of science for protection and prevention of the contagion.

During the lockdown, the stay-at-home order in many great cities of the world, ordinary citizens have learned how to keep hope and also humor alive while following the physical-separation rules necessary to defeat the virus, and then to seek to be thankful. I was so inspired when I watched what happened in Milan, Italy, as citizens sang each afternoon from their balconies. Similarly, Paul calls for the Christians at Ephesus to "make melody" to the Lord. Because of our Lord's love and truth, we have the right to claim hope and love in gratitude "at all times." The power of evil forces can be overcome.

As believers, we need to trust in the goodness and Lordship of Jesus Christ, and to claim his strength, so we can stand our ground in the face of all forces and all kinds of wrongness. Paul is not afraid of evil, either spiritual or earthbound, and now the Christians at Ephesus—and we as believers today—need to have the right equipment for such a danger and time of stress.

> 6:13–17 *Therefore take up the whole armor of God, so that you may be able to withstand on that evil day, and having done everything, to stand firm. Stand therefore, and fasten the belt of truth around your waist, and put on the breastplate of righteousness. As shoes for your feet put on whatever will make you ready to proclaim the gospel of peace. With all of these, take the shield of faith, with which you will be able to quench all the flaming arrows of the evil one. Take the helmet of salvation, and the sword of the Spirit, which is the word of God.*

---

*The armor of God is capable of both defending and protecting with the features of truth, righteousness, peace, faith, salvation, and the presence of the Lord, as assured by his words.*

---

## SECTION III: PAUL OFFERS ADVICE FOR THE PEOPLE OF THE GOSPEL

Paul next lists the necessary equipment. He begins with a belt to bind or gird our loins. He is describing a belt buckled around our waist, and **that belt is truth**. The belt of truth is the first item on the equipment list. I have a personal experience with equipment that helps me understand Paul's whole armor-of-God analogy. When I was pastor at First Presbyterian Church of Berkeley from 1970 to 1991, I was a close friend of the team physician of the Golden Bear football team of U. C. Berkeley, Dr. Jerry Patmont.[5] I was honored for a few years to meet informally with members of the team and a few coaches of our team on home game mornings. It was a time the team called morning chapel. We met at the Hotel Claremont, Berkeley, where the team would spend the Friday night before the Saturday 1:00 p.m. game in Memorial Stadium. I naturally arrived early and watched the team prepare for the day's game. The largest assembly room at the hotel was committed as a taping room; each player, with members of the trainer staff, was taping. As far as I could tell, every player's ankles and lower legs and sometimes waists and shoulders had to be taped. It became clear to me that this taping was of vital importance. It protected from sprains and gave added protection to the athletes' loins, legs, and feet.

St. Paul was not aware of the role that locker room taping would play for young athletes, but he does make the belt of truth the essential part of the whole armor that holds everything together, not unlike the tape. "The truth" is that tape that is belted on early, to make possible the other key parts of the whole.

In this parable about armor, truth emerges as the enabling power. The "truth" of a game, with its rules and agreed-upon boundaries, makes a game possible. The belt of truth also holds in place every separate piece, even including shoes, of the uniform. Tape protects the skin from chafing, scratches, and irritation from movable parts of the player's uniform. Therefore St. Paul, like a wise coach, identifies the belt of truth first of all. That belt can help us

---

5. Jerome H. Patmont (1925–2006) was head team physician for the intercollegiate Sports Program at the University of California, Berkeley. He was honored in the Cal Athletic Hall of Fame.

## PART 9: STAND WITH STRENGTH

to recognize that falsehoods can never hold us together, and Paul shows the gospel's natural and vital alliance with all truth.

This is followed by protection for the most vulnerable middle part of the body, where heart, spleen, and lungs need protection to sustain a healthy body during stresses and sudden assaults. Paul here places **the breastplate of righteousness**. This piece of equipment needs to provide freedom of movement, along with a strong yet lightweight outer cover. The word for "righteousness" is *dikaios*. This often-used New Testament word is translated in two ways. It is the word for "just right," and therefore it is a freedom word in the New Testament. It also is the justice word, depending on the need of a sentence. The "making right" word, therefore, is translated both ways in English: "righteousness" and "justification." This breastplate signifies both the freedom of "just rightness" and the restoration of "justice." "Just right" means that we are set free to move as is needed and right. It also is a word that goes with forgiveness, which makes space if injury may occur. It provides a protective, healing space so an athlete can still function, even if injured, and it helps prevent further harm. That is the role of the breastplate of righteousness.

Paul then moves his attention to the all-important mobility of our feet: **fitting our feet with readiness for the gospel of peace**. There is in Paul's armor no offensive goal for the equipment/armor; instead, he makes the goal of this analogy for Christians to be able to walk or even run forward, with readiness (*hetoimazo*) to move. This word appears more than forty times in the New Testament as being "ready to spring into action" for the gospel of peace, walking or running toward the peacemaker task with the good news of grace. The fully engaged and ready man or woman now has armor that is flexible and mobile, ready to walk or run. Every mountaineer knows that keeping your feet blister-free and protected from frostbite is the number one key rule on a snowy peak, as it is in the forward action noted in this whole analogy of readiness: be ready with good news of peace.

"Besides all these take up **the shield of faith**." The *thureos* was a narrow, oblong shield. The purpose of the shield was to be defensive and handle the flaming arrows, *belos*, "darts or arrows" of "the evil one." We should not overrate the firepower of evil; its fire can be extinguished (quenched), as Paul now promises, because our faith in the faithfulness of God makes our prayers to the Lord for his help effective. God always pays close attention. Furthermore, the shield is a moveable piece of equipment, offering the protection of trust in the faithfulness and resourcefulness of God, regardless of the evil one's angle of attack.

Then Paul adds **the helmet of salvation**, *soterios*. This word is "safety," or "to be safe," or "saving preservation" as its primary meaning. The part of the body we instinctually seek to protect at all costs is our head. Now, we have a helmet that keeps our head safe. This piece of equipment, salvation, keeps us safe in the context of the threat in that our faith in Christ carries the promise of deliverance from sin and the consequences of sin. Paul recognizes that we have to keep our heads clear and not become a victim of anxieties, conspiracy thoughts, or other worries.

The final piece of equipment is a sword, but not a warrior's sword of steel. It is **the sword of the spirit, which is the word of God**. This final part of the whole equipment is profoundly positive, not aggressive but powerful, because Paul equates the word of God with the word by which God as Creator said, "Let there be light" (Gen 1:3). This light reflects the word of forgiveness that comes in the Jesus of Nazareth. During his ministry, and even in his gravest hour at the cross, Jesus prayed to his Father, "Father, forgive them." This is the word of saving grace. Also at the cross, Jesus spoke the greatest possible word to a man condemned as a thief, who said to Jesus—as our Lord was also a man condemned—"Jesus, remember me when you come into your kingdom." Jesus replied, "Amen I tell you, today you will be with me in Paradise" (Luke 23:42–43). The Lord has given us his love, and he has spelled out in words how we are to share this love.

> 6:18–20 *Pray in the Spirit at all times in every prayer and supplication. To that end keep alert and always persevere in supplication for all the saints. Pray also for me, so that when I speak, a message may be given to me to make*

PART 9: STAND WITH STRENGTH

*known with boldness the mystery of the gospel, for which I am an ambassador in chains. Pray that I may declare it boldly, as I must speak.*

This man who met the Lord Jesus on the road to Damascus concludes his teaching with a request of his friends in Ephesus. He asks them to stay in the Spirit and stay wide awake as they pray for all the saints. He also asks for their prayers for himself: "Pray also for me . . . when I speak . . ." He asks for boldness so that he will be able to share the mystery of the gospel. Paul is an ambassador in chains but still able to speak, and on that ambassadorial note, he ends his teaching.

## Ephesians 6:21–24

### Words of Farewell that Encourage

[21] So that you also may know how I am and what I am doing, Tychicus will tell you everything. He is a dear brother and a faithful minister in the Lord. [22] I am sending him to you for this very purpose, to let you know how we are, and to encourage your hearts. [23] Peace be to the brothers and sisters, and love with faith, from God the Father and the Lord Jesus Christ. [24] Grace be with all who have an undying love for our Lord Jesus Christ.

In these closing words, Paul, the man from Tarsus, leaves it for his friend Tychius to carry a personal greeting to first-century Christians—and also to us in the twenty-first century.

*6:21, 22 So that you also may know how I am and what I am doing, Tychicus will tell you everything. He is a dear brother and a **faithful minister in the Lord**. I am sending him to you for this very purpose, to let you know how we are, and to encourage your hearts.*

Paul began Ephesians with the words "Grace to you and peace" (Eph 1:2) and now his closing words bring his message full circle.

## SECTION III: PAUL OFFERS ADVICE FOR THE PEOPLE OF THE GOSPEL

> 6:23, 24 *Peace be to the brothers and sisters, and love with faith, from God the Father and the Lord Jesus Christ. Grace be with all who have an undying love for our Lord Jesus Christ.*

How significant that this man from Tarsus ends his letter with the same important words that he used to begin. Paul wants **peace** for them, as it represents wholeness. He wants **love** for them, because it represents not an idea but an event. He wants **grace** for them, because it represents an event that was unexpected. And joy!

# Postscript

*The question that I have asked myself is "How is this book by Paul useful for us at this time of history?"*

As I have immersed myself in the study of Ephesians over this past year, I am drawn to Paul's realistic optimism in the face of his circumstances. His centered faith brings hope for the world in the face of whatever conditions seem to prevail. Paul calls each one of us to invite God's presence into our lives and to stand with the truth of God's power of love. As I see it, we need to listen to these words today—in a world under the public stress of threat posed by the COVID pandemic with the fear it brings and the personal stress of suspicion elevated within the human family that divides and brings harm one to another.

In the center of this letter is a basic and simple prayer that has endured. "I bow my knees before the Father . . . that Christ may dwell in your hearts through faith; that you, being rooted and grounded in love, may have power to comprehend . . . what is the breadth and length and height and depth, and to know the love of Christ . . . that you may be filled with all the fullness of God" (Eph 3:14-19). With these words Paul establishes the reality of Jesus Christ, who showed that his love is the truth that holds us together. He explains what he believes—that the love of Christ within us can expand our comprehension of that which surrounds us. He encourages to seek truth in all things.

Paul unites the themes of his letter with a challenge. "I therefore, a prisoner of the Lord beg you to lead a life *worthy* of the calling to which you have been called with lowliness and meekness, with patience, lifting up one another in love, eager to maintain the unity of the spirit in the bond of peace" (Eph 4:1–3). Knowing the truth has the power to anchor us. This word "worthy," translated from the Greek *axios*, signifies a self-authenticated truth that provides a steadying resource by which to live. The presence of the Lord takes away fear and helps us to stand. Knowing this love guides us so that we can reach out to others with confidence.

*The mystery of Christ* (Eph 3:4) is not a mystery of cultic conspiratorial secrets but the mystery made known because of Christ's love. He loves each of us and all of us together. He has broken down all dividing walls so that we all may become fellow heirs, members of the same body, and share in the promise in Christ through the gospel. All human relationships are mediated by the love of Jesus, who is in between and in our favor. This truth helps us to see those we now know and those we do not know in a different light. Jesus really lived, and Jesus paid a price that all of us in the human family might live in the light of Christ's love. This truth steadied him, and it promises to steady us.

Paul calls us to be alert and stand in the middle of the swirling winds. He wants us to recognize there are "winds" of competing views, misinformation, and even beliefs that can be based on falsehood that swirl around us and threaten our balance. He describes these winds. He gives examples of practical discipleship of behaviors "to put off" and "to put on." He tells us not to yield to that which creates harm to self and to others; to be aware when situations emerge that do not embrace truth. He reminds us to remember the rule of love toward self and neighbor, and to act with the steadying presence of the living Christ, which gives power to truth. This truth of the love that flows from the Lord through his life, death, and resurrection is the *axios*—the truth filled with grace, which protects us from temptations and pathways of deception.

As the Letter to the Ephesians comes to a close Paul uses a parable to explain what we need to do to protect ourselves and to counter pathways that can lead to harm. He gives a listing of the whole armor of God to enable us to stand with strength when we face windy landscapes of dangerous threats that isolate and try to put us out of action when we are needed to be present and alert.

## POSTSCRIPT

In this time in which I now live, I am encouraged by the letter from Paul to trust in the love that is described through the life, death, and resurrection of Jesus Christ, and what it means for each one of us. And to find assurance in knowing that this love holds promise for life and it is for us and for us to share. St. Paul has helped me to recognize that there are factors present that can set us off balance, and to know that truth has the power to withstand the turbulence. And finally, I am inspired to practice the way of living that gives witness to this truth and love.

And now, may we go forth with grace and be at peace: steadied by the truth of Christ who loves us; called to be a people of the gospel and share that love. I commend the warmhearted words of Paul to you.

Your brother in Christ,
Earl

# Appendix I: **Resource for Expositional Preaching and Teaching**

[This article appeared in *Preaching Today/Christianity Today* (May, 2019) and offers some concrete steps to follow when doing an exposition of a biblical text.]

### Then Something Happened

The Case for Exposition of the Bible

*By Rev. Earl F. Palmer*

Then something happened, something that has changed and transformed my life to the present day. For the first time I discovered the Bible... Since then everything has changed. I have felt this plainly, and so have other people around me. It was a great liberation.

—Dietrich Bonhoeffer[1]

THE BIBLE BECAME A book I really wanted to read during my sophomore year at U.C. Berkeley. It was there in Barrington Hall, a large student co-op, at a weekly student-led Bible discussion group that the random pieces of my worldview began to come together. It was there that my discovery of the Jesus Christ of the Bible made all the difference. A new wholeness began to take shape for me. At the end of that academic year I went to a retreat at Lake Tahoe with some of my friends from that Bible Study and I heard the

---

1. Bethge, *Dietrich Bonhoeffer*, 205. These are the opening comments by Bonhoeffer who wrote these words in a letter to a friend in 1936.

Rev. Dr. Robert Boyd Munger, pastor of First Presbyterian Church of Berkeley, speak. He said one sentence during the Bible Study that caught my full attention. "If on the basis of the evidence of what you now know about Jesus Christ you are willing to trust in his trustworthiness, then you are on your way to becoming a Christian believer." Because of what I had learned from the Bible I did just that—I put my trust in Jesus Christ.

## The Bible as Witness

Who is this Jesus Christ? He is the Jesus of history to whom the Bible points to in the Old Testament by its own story and anticipation, and in the New Testament through its witness to the fulfillment of the ancient prophets and songs. If I agree that Jesus of Nazareth is the Christ in whom I trust and follow, I have joined myself to the Bible and to biblical faith. To quote Joachim Jeremais, "Every verse of the Gospels tells us that the origin of Christianity is not the kerygma, not the resurrection experience of the disciples, not the Christ idea, but an historical event, to wit, the appearance of the man, Jesus of Nazareth."[2]

The Old Testament prepares an ordinary reader to meet Jesus of the first century and to discover his story in the narratives of New Testament writers. My attention turns to the New Testament. When I reflect upon how I came to consider the story about Jesus I can understand that it is a journey. One can begin with serious reservations, even skeptically. Nevertheless, sooner or later a person is drawn into the accounts of the life of Jesus with the realization that "Matthew, whoever he is, tells about Jesus." Mark, Luke, and John also tell of Jesus' works, his ministry, his death and his victory over death. For me as I read on to the letters Paul wrote to believers throughout the first-century world, I began to see more parts of the puzzle come together, showing who the person of Jesus Christ is.

---

2. Jeremais, "Present Position in the Controversy," 333. Jeremias is always clear and to the point.

APPENDIX I: RESOURCE FOR EXPOSITIONAL PREACHING AND TEACHING

Whether gradually or quickly, this New Testament Jesus wins me to Himself. He gains my respect, my trust, my faith. Karl Barth writes, "Holy Scripture is the document of the basis, of the innermost life of the Church, the document of the manifestation of the Word of God in the person of Jesus Christ. We have no other document for the living basis of the Church."[3] What I learn about Jesus makes sense to my complete being—intellectually, spiritually and emotionally.

This happened to me. After the retreat I returned to Berkeley and became more active in the Barrington study group. I saw men discover Jesus, and one by one become Christians. The Lord honored that small Bible study group. I was so turned on by what was happening and by my experiences in our Christian fellowship that in the middle of my senior year, I took a leap from my pre-law, political science major. I approached Rev. Robert Munger with a question, "You know, I wonder if I could be a minister?" He replied, "Why don't you apply to a seminary and see?" So I applied to Princeton Theological Seminary. I am sure that I was the greenest recruit they had for that year, 1953.

Princeton was a renaissance experience. I discovered John A. MacKay, a great biblical preacher with the world on his heart. His way of preaching became a model to me. Along with fellow seminarians, I started Bible study groups across campus with young men at Princeton University. As I watched students discover Jesus through these Bible studies, just as I did at Berkeley, I learned that if I could encourage people to read the biblical text, it would do its own convincing. Blaise Pascal reminds us, "People are generally better persuaded by the reasons which they have discovered than by those which have come into the mind of others."[4] Since that time I have centered my pastoral teaching ministry upon this basic premise in Seattle, Manila, Berkeley and Washington, D.C.

---

3. Barth, *Dogmatics in Outline*, 40. Barth's first three chapters in this book are a very helpful introduction to biblical theology.

4. Pascal, *Pensées*, 7. Pascal (1623–1662) has a lasting power to inspire and turn our eyes towards Jesus Christ.

## APPENDIX I: RESOURCE FOR EXPOSITIONAL PREACHING AND TEACHING

I define this undertaking as exposition: a teaching/preaching form that enables a text in the Old and/or New Testament to make its own point here and now, and, in turn, positions the content of the text within the whole biblical and theological witness to the gospel of Jesus Christ. Exposition of the biblical text becomes a natural way to make a theological and discipleship truth relevant and allows people to discover it for themselves. The goal is to help a person meet this Jesus and be able to say, "Ah, I see the truth for myself in the portrayal of the life of Jesus." For me personally, I have found that a small group who study the Bible together is a perfect setting for exposition.

### How to Prepare for Exposition

Exposition of the biblical text is fundamental to my call as preaching pastor in Christian ministry. The question is, "How then do I prepare for this kind of preaching/teaching as a working pastor?" In brief, I have learned that the place to begin is to write your own commentary on the biblical texts under study/consideration. There are five steps I use to guide me with questions to ask in this approach.

#### *Establish the text*

This begins with learning what is the context/background for the language/words used in the text. The types of questions include:

- Who is the writer?
- What is the date of the writing?
- Who are the first receivers of the writing?

The tools to find answers are universally available and applicable. Searching for this information means access to a good library. I use *The International Dictionary of the Bible* (4 volumes). I recommend Hasting's *Dictionary of the Bible*. I suggest doing your own study in the original language texts using Greek and Hebrew lexicons such as *Theological Dictionary of the Old Testament* and *Theological Dictionary of the New Testament.*

It is important to pay attention to the extensive and rich resources in the many different English translations of the Bible available today. I advise using a minimum of five different translations to see how various translators handle the text. Examples include *The New RSV, NIV, American Standard Version, the Jerusalem Bible,* and *The Message* (contemporary). Watch as translators endeavor to establish the best English rendering of the Greek/Hebrew text.

This is the interpretive journey that requires careful reading to seek the meanings of the sentences and especially the meanings of the words used. Ask:

- How were the words understood in the first century?
- Why is one word used instead of another?

For word study specifically I like *The Eerdman's Analytical Concordance to the Revised Standard Version of The Bible.*

*Focus on the historical setting of the text itself*

Consider:

- What might a news reporter discover with questions about time, place, people, atmosphere, and crises present or about to happen?
- Are there interior clues about why the book was written?
- What problems are surfaced in the material/content itself?

Background books and dictionaries of the Bible as an aid here are essential. A helpful and broad overview is *The International Standard Bible Encyclopedia* (4 volumes). But the key to discovery is your own inquisitiveness.

APPENDIX I: RESOURCE FOR EXPOSITIONAL PREACHING AND TEACHING

*Determine the meaning and purpose of the text*

Figure out:

- What do the words say?
- What do the words mean?

This leads to the theological content questions. C. S. Lewis put it this way: "Find out what the author actually wrote and what the hard words meant and what the allusions were to, and you have done far more for me than a hundred new interpretations... could ever do."[5] It is prudent to move slowly and carefully to learn from the whole context of the book and keep asking

- What is the writer saying and why?

The general rule I follow is that the meaning of each separate part is principally governed by the meaning of the larger part. For example, to find the meaning of one sentence by Saint Paul I must look to that sentence's larger paragraph, then to the collections of paragraphs, even other books written by Paul. For instance, read how St. Paul in 1 Corinthians 13 frames the concept of "love" as a greater truth than the lesser value of "speaking with the tongues of men and angels."

*Get information on the relevance to the present*

Expand inquiry to the present:

- What are the challenges, even dangers that threaten faith within the church that receives the document?

This question unfolds the contemporary significance. For example, notice how Paul teaches about first century dangers of harmful tribalism (Romans 12, Ephesians 2) or learn from the Lord's Sermon on the Mount (Matthew 5–7). How are these teachings

---

5. Lewis, *Experiment in Criticism*, 121. This is Lewis's book about how to read a book. I think it is one of the best aids to Bible study I know.

## APPENDIX I: RESOURCE FOR EXPOSITIONAL PREACHING AND TEACHING

relevant to twenty-first century problems of tribalism and hatreds between people? Biblical exposition opens up situations to deliberate in our present century just as it did in the first century and is thus useful for guidance and understanding the "now."

### *Understand how the text applies to discipleship*

These questions include:

- What does this text say to me?
- What are the implications for my life?

In every study of the Bible we must always include ourselves and try to understand the ramifications of the teaching on choices we make daily in what we do and how we do it. The best teaching uses "we" language more than "they" or "you" language. To understand the personal impact of the passage, I need to include myself as a learner in this whole journey/quest.

These five general steps take time but they are essential in the preparation for the teaching and preaching tasks of the pastor. This work of sharing the discoveries of the study of texts sets the tone for worship. When I prepare a sermon I always ask these types of questions of the biblical text. I look first for logical connections or the progressions in meanings that enable me to make two or three or even four observations from the interpretation of the text. In so doing my sermon outline is underway!

Additionally, I like to add windows into the main discovery points. These windows come in the form of illustrations, and are often present within the story elements of a text itself. An illustration might come from my own life, or from the literature I read. The right illustration helps to make a truth clear. What helps me is to ask these types of questions of the text:

- What is this like?
- What is what I read in the text similar to something I know about?

The preaching goal is to conclude the sermon quickly when major discoveries from the text are hopefully made understandable. It is important to allow the power of the text to stand without elaborate and extensive closing comments by the preacher. Martin Luther was an inspiration to me in his *Lectures on Romans*. He would explain a meaningful part of a text from Paul and then say, "That's enough for today." I try not to be that abrupt but yet in that spirit—exposition at its best happens when that the listener has an "ah-ha" moment and sees for himself or herself what the text says and means. At such moments as the preacher I am not needed to over-interpret or insist on my own final summary of the meaning.

## The Pastoral Mandate in Preaching

The use of a single biblical text selected out of context to promote a particular idea is a temptation in pastoral leadership and preaching. The downside can be sometimes described as a thematic domination of the sermons. While the themes may honor and include biblical references, the key source of the message can be the pastor's own personal life experiences, convictions of faith, and even political outlook. When this happens, a subtle shift in the sermon's validating affirmation moves into the territory of story/platform rather than a message from the text. The message can morph into the claim that "you should have hope or love or an ethical concern because I do."

Rather than relying on the learning from the expanse of the biblical text the source of the message is contained/restricted. The pastor's own personal issues can become the practical source of the message because the choice of theme is managed and controlled by a previously decided agenda. This can result in a thematic captivity of a preaching goal. To counter this possibility is to engage in thoughtful study of texts where the biblical witness has its chance with our minds.

Along this same line of thinking I want to also raise a related question, "Is my own experience of blessings and inspiration from the Holy Spirit the appropriate/proper instructional guideline

## APPENDIX I: RESOURCE FOR EXPOSITIONAL PREACHING AND TEACHING

that gives broad authoritative importance for those I serve as a pastor/teacher?" This is not to discount my life experiences nor undervalue lessons that support truth and provide windows of encouragement. However, I need to recognize that my story is not of the same weight as the word of the Lord in the gospel, which is sourced in Jesus Christ's life and teachings.

I am called to faithfully preach the gospel as derived from life of Jesus. The weight is on the gospel. It is not within my purview to claim that my experiences and viewpoint hold the authority or preach authoritative guidance for living. The mandate is to point to Jesus Christ. I am called to make the life of Jesus knowable as the gospel reveals and open a door for people to discover through their own personal lens the meaning for themselves.

I do not dispute that the sharing of personal stories in preaching can be vital. The preacher is a human being and sees through a personally influenced lens that can become a key ingredient in the making of a sermon and can connect with every listener who also sees and experiences life through a personally influenced lens. God's grace in our lives does not cancel out the channel of human influences. Rather we are enriched and made more alive and able to focus on the grace of God at work; it helps our sense of being human too. I only suggest such sharing not be the focus, that it be tempered.

Again, please understand, this is not to diminish the sharing of personal stories as illustrations to support the text. It is just not the central message/main focus to be delivered from the pulpit. As a pastor it requires a humility and explanation that restrains me so I can speak to the central message in the biblical text that tells of the life of Christ.

This thinking also applies to the telling of harmful life experiences and suggesting final permanence as if the negative is the last word. Every human story is a mid-story. The Lord of the good news stands alongside and his grace is beyond our own mid-story conclusions. This basic understanding/theology undergirds the role of the pastor to serve as the under-shepherd of the people with hope for the future. The premise is that the last word belongs to Jesus Christ.

APPENDIX I: RESOURCE FOR EXPOSITIONAL PREACHING AND TEACHING

## The Bible Rightly Honored

Dorothy L. Sayers writes, "The Christian faith is the most exciting drama that ever staggered the imagination . . . The plot pivots upon a single character, and the whole action is the answer to a single central problem: 'What think ye of Christ?'"[6] We worship Jesus Christ, not the Holy Bible. The Bible, taken seriously, never stimulates false worship, but through its texts and themes, its history and poetry, its yearnings and prayers, the narratives of real people from Moses to John, the Bible always finally points us to its Lord of the text: The Old Testament by anticipation, the New Testament in witness.

Because of the timelessness of Jesus Christ himself, the Bible's witness to his ministry is across generations and multicultural. Biblical faith does not blunt our ability to be a wise and streetwise observer of the contemporary scene. I believe the healthy pressure of the gospel rather creates just the opposite result—a sharpened sensitivity and inquisitiveness that grows out of a stance toward life that does not need to fear truth wherever we find it.

There is one word of caution. A doctrinal wanderlust can sometimes take hold of a student of the Bible. It may create its own momentum, and with it an insatiable appetite for the new and the different. This wanderlust should not be confused with the research instinct that we have been describing, or the hard work of theological inquiry and honest debate about meanings and teachings. The restlessness in research is founded upon the whole principle of testing followed by meaningful response to truth discovered. Wanderlust is not freedom, though it may disguise itself as freedom, but often it results in an intellectual, moral and spiritual loneliness.

I can think of no more exciting task in our age, so often adrift, and yet underneath it all so hungry for the real, than to have the privilege of sharing in the witness to Jesus Christ, the same yesterday, today, and tomorrow. It is the biblical text of the life of Jesus

---

6. Sayers, *Christian Letters to a Post-Christian World*, 13. See also her brilliant war-time BBC broadcast drama *The Man Born to be King*.

that brought the young pastor, Dietrich Bonhoeffer, to write these words that offer a steadying hope:

> "Let the word of Christ dwell in you richly" (Col. 3:16). The Old Testament day begins at evening and ends with the going down of the sun. It is the time of expectation. The day of the New Testament church begins with the break of day and ends with the dawning of light of the next morning. It is the time of fulfillment, the resurrection of the Lord. At night Christ was born, a light in the darkness; noonday turned to night when Christ suffered and died on the Cross. But in the dawn of Easter morning Christ rose in victory from the grave.[7]

---

7. Bonhoeffer, *Life Together*, 40. The brief book was the result of his experience at the informal confessing pastors' lived-in seminars at Finkenwald.

# Appendix II: Reflections on the Life of Paul of Tarsus

How did a Roman citizen from a prominent Jewish family, highly educated and privileged to study under a famous teacher, a moderate Pharisee, become radicalized and a dangerous opponent of the followers of the risen Rabbi Jesus?

What influenced Saul/Paul that made him engage in actions that harmed others—even to the death of a young deacon named Stephen?

What happened on the road to Damascus that brought Saul/Paul out of the darkness of his intense persecution of the early Christians to the place of enlightenment of faith and grace?

What words would you use to describe Jesus' encounter with Saul/Paul on the road to Damascus?

Can you explain what Jesus meant when he said to Saul/Paul that "it hurts to kick against the goads"?

What role does the church in Damascus play in relating to Paul after his encounter with Jesus?

What are the reasons for the early advice from Barnabas given to Paul, a new Christian, to return to Tarsus?

## APPENDIX II: REFLECTIONS ON THE LIFE OF PAUL OF TARSUS

In what way does the interaction with the people of the church in Damascus become marks of a gospel destiny for Paul?

What attributes describe Paul as a changed person after his experience in meeting Christ and in being cared for by the people of the gospel in Damascus?

How are the influences of the people in Damascus revealed later in Paul's teaching?

How would you describe Paul's journey of teaching and preaching throughout the province of Asia and the whole of the Mediterranean world?

What words would you use to define the main message of Paul's life?

What clues do you find that explain Paul's resilience to survive in his times of imprisonment?

How did Paul's experience of grace allow him to offer grace to those in his surroundings?

# Appendix III: Reflections on the Letter to the Ephesians

**1:1–8** Paul begins all of his letters with the words "grace" and "peace." In Ephesians he adds the word "blessed," that is translated from the Greek word *eulogos* (the good word).

> In what ways does this word "blessing" signal important fulfillment themes for the people?

**1:9–23** In this section, Paul uses the dramatic word *apocalypsis* here as he did in Romans 1:17.

> Does the use of this word surprise you?
>
> Compare the text in *Ephesians 1:17* with the text in *Romans 1:17*.
>
> Why you think Paul uses the word *apocalypsis* in both of these texts?
>
> Why does Paul focus on this word *apocalypsis*?
>
> What happens that helps Paul become aware that a battle has been won on our behalf that brings fulfillment in human destiny?

**2:1–3** Paul interrupts the grand positive vision of the prayer to draw attention to the wrongness of human trespasses and sins. Paul includes himself in the list with "all of us." In so doing, he

## APPENDIX III: REFLECTIONS ON THE LETTER TO THE EPHESIANS

reveals the intense desires that can result in harm of our own personal ambitions and goals.

> Why does Paul offer this stark insight into our desires that can become extreme and wrathful toward ourselves and others?

*2:3-4* (See also 2 Timothy 2:22-25.) As he did in his 2 Timothy, Paul exposes the dangers of religious and secular strong desire for power.

> What are some reasons that Paul includes such concrete dangers to the integrity and moral character of those who seek to follow Jesus but instead adopt behaviors that are against what God intends to be the way of life?
>
> If Paul's comments have merit, how is it that believers in Christ who claim his love are deceived and justify pathways of wrath/vengeance and cruelty?
>
> Can redemption happen for Christians who have become caught up in the ways of evil? Explain.

*2:4-10* Paul welcomes new believers into the household of God because of their trust in Jesus Christ and in so doing expands the promise of the "heavenly inheritance" to all who believe.

> How do you explain the simplified route that Paul gives as the way of healing that he describes as "by grace, not of your own doing"?

*2:11-13* Paul asserts that simple trust in Christ is all that we need to be in the presence of the Lord. This foundation of truth does not rest on ceremony, tradition, or religious rituals.

> How do you understand the ancient sign of the covenant, the rite of circumcision? What do you propose is

## APPENDIX III: REFLECTIONS ON THE LETTER TO THE EPHESIANS

the reasoning that enables Paul to grant this rite to be of secondary importance?

What then do you understand is of primary importance?

**2:14–22** (See also Acts 15: 6–10, 13–14, and 19.) Here Paul writes about the dividing walls that separate the people? The book of Acts sheds light on the way Paul describes the one body with Christ Jesus as the one who unites all people who believe. St. Luke tells of the first early church council meeting of the apostles in Jerusalem that ended well for the gospel, for future believers, and for all nations—Jews and Gentiles alike.

Can you explain how tribalism creates divisions among people? Or how the facets of the tribalism of race, religious practices, political agendas, etc. create divisions among people?

In what ways might you describe St. Paul as a non-tribalist?

**3:1–13** Paul uses the word "mystery" to describe the oneness vision of both Gentiles and Jews as a people in one fellowship who benefit from the eternal purpose of God's grace set forth in the ancient promise of the prophets and holy apostles.

How does Paul explain this mystery?

What is meant by Paul's phrase, "the purpose of God's grace"?

**1:3 to 3:21** (Summary:) The first three chapters of Ephesians are presented as a prayer. The themes in this prayer include the broad collections of moods and emotions, the disappointing failure when believers do not follow truth. But then intermittently comes the lightning clarity of grace that breaks in to interrupt the hostility caused when bitter untruths surface as if they were

## APPENDIX III: REFLECTIONS ON THE LETTER TO THE EPHESIANS

true. Then the grace and truth of Jesus as redeemer draws the prayer toward the benediction that gives hope with its grand final affirmation of the goodness of God.

> What are the main themes in this prayer?
>
> Can you explain how the many themes converge?
>
> How would you describe the final sentence of Paul's prayer as both a mystery and yet totally understandable as truth and pure music that sings?

**4:1-3** This chapter begins with "therefore," which connects all that follows to the grand prayer. The words in the English Bible are translated in most texts as "Lead a life worthy of the calling." The actual Greek word in the text for worthy is *axios*. I interpret *axios* as "steadied." It is through the discovery of God's truth and grace that we are steadied as expressed in Paul's language of prayer in the first three chapters. The permanent truth of the prayer is self-authenticated.

> How and in what ways does *axios*/truth steady the lives and behavior choices of a believer?

Paul lists four virtues of character that flow from the truth of God's love: (1) humility (2) gentleness (3) patience (4) bearing one another's burdens.

> How do these virtues speak to what Paul has in mind as his wish for friends at Ephesus?

**4:4-5** In this text we actually encounter a brief notation of the meaning of the rite of baptism. This is Paul's only actual mention of baptism in Ephesians.

> How would you summarize Paul's teaching concerning the rite of baptism?

***4:14*** Paul alerts to the Ephesian Christians who are facing strong winds of temptation. He uses two words and both are part of the temptation narrative. The first is *kubei*—trickery is the interpretation of the Greek word "dice" in most translations. The second is *planao*—translated as "deceive," which has a similar meaning of "misleading."

> What do you think are Paul's concerns as he gives the warning of "being tossed to and fro and carried about with every wind of doctrine, by the cunning of man, by their craftiness to deceitful wiles"?
>
> How does God's truth steady the believers who face different forms of deception?

***4:15-16*** Here is a discipleship text with two important messages. First, Paul returns to his earlier word use of the Greek word *synarnologeo* in Ephesians 2:21 that brings together the concept of the joining together in a meaningful place—of bringing the people of faith into the dwelling place for God. Now in Ephesians 4:16 he uses this word again to say that as the people of God we are joined together into the body of Christ where each part promotes the body's growth in building itself up in love.

A second word with Paul's use of *epichorogus* builds from the musical word "chorus" to show how comfort is choreographed by God's design to/for our benefit. He highlights the "knitting together" of every part to the fulfillment of the love of God.

> How does this explanation enrich your understanding of discipleship?

***4: 17-19*** This section presents a downward path into darkness that descends with words of futility: shadows, hardness of heart, loss of human empathy, reckless moral behavior. Compare Romans 8, where help is given in the face of the dangers of futility?

## APPENDIX III: REFLECTIONS ON THE LETTER TO THE EPHESIANS

What do you think Paul intended by giving this harsh list? Why would Paul want to address behaviors that do not endure but are futile?

**4:20-32** These texts make clear that discipleship is a journey of deciding on the part of a follower of Jesus. Paul chooses a word game to reveal this strategy.

How can Paul's approach be helpful for decision-making and choice of actions as a growing Christian?

What are some of the ways Christians are led away from God's truth and truthfulness in favor of falsehoods that appear on the surface to offer advantage?

How does Paul's list of discipleship decisions offer protection against temptation?

**5:1** Paul continues to give practical advice on how to live as Christians.

How do you interpret the word "imitate" in the context of this text?

Why is it that Paul gives an exhortation to copy and model the good we see in other faithful believers?

Can you give examples of where a positive model of Christian character influenced you to act for the good?

**5:6-21** Pay attention to the long list of behaviors to "put off" and a long list of behaviors to "put on" that Paul gives in this section.

What does Paul mean with the words, "Sleeper awake! Rise from the dead, and Christ will shine on you"?

**5:21-33** In this long text, Paul acknowledges the mutual and joyous place of marriage in which the relationship of two is held together in the post or station that is undergirded by God and carries responsibility to our role in history.

> How do you explain this mixture of our choice of each other and God's blessing?

> In what way do Paul's words help to preserve the joy and equal respect theme of the unique person as single and yet two together at a post that is rooted/grounded in God's love?

**6:1–9** The word "listen" becomes a key word in this discussion of the relationship of fathers with children, between slave owners and slaves.

> What examples can you give as the key concept in these relationships?

> Explain your understanding of the two ways to listen.

> How does this understanding offer restraint against human leadership in the case of wrong and unrighteous commands and communication?

> Can you think of ways that the biblical perspective of listening has become a part of standards in just and humane law?

**6:10–20** The reality of evil is discussed by Paul near the close of the letter. He gives practical advice. The armor of God emphasizes the protection that the believer has against the darts of evil.

> How does Paul help us to understand both the reality of spiritual darkness and the actuality of the inner weakness that can be activated in positions of power?

> What can be said of actions/activities that are contrary to justice and the possible consequences of doing wrong versus doing right?

## APPENDIX III: REFLECTIONS ON THE LETTER TO THE EPHESIANS

How much weight should we give to the temptation of power by the devil?

Why is it important to not over-weigh the power of the evil one?

How does Paul suggest that the act of trusting in truth can equip a believer?

What is the offensive strategy in the armor of God that Paul gives in his lists of equipment?

What do you see as the benefits of each of the elements described as protection against the evil one? Discuss each part of the armor suggested by Paul.

**6:21–24** Paul ends his letter somewhat suddenly. Yet he comes full circle and closes his letter as he began with the affirmation of "Peace to the brethren, and love with faith from God the Father and the Lord Jesus Christ and grace be with all who love our Lord Jesus Christ with love undying."

Why might Paul be abrupt in ending this letter?

Can you describe what you think Paul was feeling/expressing when he said to Timothy, "Do your best to come to me soon. . . . When you come, bring the cloak . . . , also the books, and above all, the parchments. . . . Do your best to come before winter (2 Timothy 4:9, 13, & 21).

What thoughts went through your mind when you read the words in Acts 20:36–38 that end with "And they brought him to the ship . . ."?

How do you explain the unexpected ending Paul has in a letter to his friends in Ephesus?

Could there be some purpose in Paul telling the Ephesians about his messenger, Tychius?

## APPENDIX III: REFLECTIONS ON THE LETTER TO THE EPHESIANS

Read Paul's final letter in 2 Timothy 4:6–8 and consider his words, "I have fought the good fight . . ."

In your own words describe what you believe to be the challenges of being a believer in today's world.

What aspects of Paul's life and testimony are most memorable to you and inspire you "to lead a life worthy of the calling"?

# Appendix IV: Strategies to Follow in Small Group Bible Studies

## A Personal Note

I have learned from Bonhoeffer's approach to Bible study. He would ask questions of the text as the words unfolded. His Introduction to *The Cost of Discipleship* gives an example of his approach in exposition of biblical themes. Notice how he begins his study of the call to discipleship with questions. In so doing, he offers clues for how to approach exposition of a biblical text.

> And if we answer the call to discipleship, where will it lead us? What decisions and partings will it demand? To answer this question we shall have to go to him, for only he knows the answer. Only Jesus Christ, who bids us follow him, knows the journey's end. But we do know that it will be a road of boundless mercy. Discipleship means joy.[1]

In my experience when people study the Bible, they are able to make the discovery of Jesus Christ and the meaning of that discovery for their own lives. I am an advocate for small group Bible studies during which questions can be raised and answers found. Permit me to offer a few guidelines that have helped me in my own study and my experience with small groups. I would encourage you to ask questions in your study of the Letter to the Ephesians. Questions can help each of us as we seek to live our lives and answer the call to be a people of the gospel.

---

1. Bonhoeffer, *Cost of Discipleship*, 32.

## Practical Strategies to Follow in Small Group Bible Studies

1. Call a group of people together for the purpose of studying the Bible.
2. Acknowledge a person as the leader who will handle the organizational details.
3. Set the date/times for the group to meet.
4. Select a reader who is willing to read aloud the specific text assigned for each meeting.
5. Recognize the leader's role to determine the places in the reading for the reader to pause and allow time for input and reflection and to also keep the discussion moving forward.
6. Consider questions such as "What are the historical anchors in terms of time, place, people for the text? Are there clues as to the immediate concerns that the anchors reveal? What can be determined about the context for the particular passage?"
7. Comment with first impressions.
8. Express your thoughts as to whether or not the writer's concerns become teaching points that encourage or are words of warning.
9. Think about how the writer draws you toward larger themes.
10. Question whether or not others in the group share similar impressions. Describe how the impressions are alike or different, and whether or not the impressions have significance to the group.
11. React to the text in terms of the discipleship questions —are there "ah-ha" moments of discovery during which the New Testament becomes important in a new way?
12. Evaluate whether the text invites further discussion.
13. End the study session with prayer requests from the group.
14. Invite an attendee to lead in prayer for God's blessing.

## APPENDIX IV: STRATEGIES TO FOLLOW IN SMALL GROUP BIBLE STUDIES

15. Remember the theme of grace and truth as you end the time together and move back into the world of work and living in the everyday.
16. Look forward to your next time when you gather together to study the Scripture.

JOY!

# References that Aided in the Study of Ephesians

Albright, William. *Recent Discoveries in Bible Lands.* New York: Funk & Wagnalls, 1955.
Arndt, William, and F. Wilbur Gingrich. *A Greek-English Lexicon of the New Testament.* Chicago: University of Chicago Press, 1955.
Barth, Karl. *Dogmatics in Outline.* New York: Harper, 1959.
Barth, Markus. *The Broken Wall: A Study of the Epistle to the Ephesians.* Valley Forge, PA: Judson, 1959.
Bethge, Eberhard. *Dietrich Bonhoeffer: A Biography.* Minneapolis: Fortress, 2000.
Bonhoeffer, Dietrich. *Letters and Papers from Prison.* Edited by Eberhard Bethge. New York: Touchstone, 1997.
———. *Life Together.* Philadelphia: Fortress, 2015.
———. *The Cost of Discipleship.* Great Britain: SCM, 1959.
Bromiley, G. W., ed. *The International Bible Encyclopedia.* Grand Rapids: Eerdmans, 1979.
Brown, Colin, ed. *New International Dictionary of New Testament Theology.* Grand Rapids: Zondervan, 1975.
Bruce, F. F., ed. *The New International Commentary on The New Testament Epistles to Colossians, Philemon, Ephesians.* Grand Rapids: Eerdmans, 1984.
Catholic Biblical Association of America. *New American Bible.* New York: Thomas Nelson, 1971.
Delegates of The Oxford University Press and The Syndics of the Cambridge University Press. *New English Bible.* Cambridge: Cambridge University Press, 1961.
Dostoyevsky, Fyodor. *The Brothers Karamazov.* New York: Oxford University Press, 1994.
Grant, Frederick, and H. H. Rowley. *Dictionary of the Bible.* Edited by James Hastings. Rev. ed. New York: Scribner, 1963.
International Bible Society. *New International Version.* Grand Rapids: Zondervan, 2005.

## REFERENCES THAT AIDED IN THE STUDY OF EPHESIANS

Jeremias, Joachim. "The Present Position in the Controversy Confronting the Problem of the Historical Jesus." *Expository Times* 69.11 (1958) 333–39.

Jones, Alexander, ed. *Jerusalem Bible*. Garden City, NY: Doubleday, 1966.

Kittel, Gerhard, ed. *Theological Dictionary of the New Testament*. Translated by G. W. Bromiley. Grand Rapids: Eerdmans, 1964.

Knox, R. A. *The New Testament: A New Translation*. New York: Sheed & Ward, 1944.

Lewis, C. S. *An Experiment in Criticism*. Cambridge: Cambridge University Press, 1961.

———. *The Screwtape Letters*. New York: Touchstone, 1961.

Mackay, John A. *God's Order: The Ephesian Letter and This Present Time*. New York: Macmillan, 1953.

Moffatt, James. *A New Translation of the Bible*. New York: Harper, 1922.

Mounce, William D., and Robert H. Mounce, eds. *Greek and English Interlinear New Testament*. Grand Rapids: Zondervan, 2008.

Pascal, Blasé. *The Pensées: Provincial Letters*. Translated by William F. Trotter and Thomas McCabe. New York: Random House, 1941.

Peterson, Eugene. *The Message*. Colorado Springs, CO: NavPress, 1993.

Sayers, Dorothy L. *Christian Letters to a Post-Christian World*. Grand Rapids: Eerdmans, 1969.

Stott, John R. W. *The Spirit, The Church and The World: The Message of Acts*. Downers Grove, IL: Intervarsity, 1990.

Tolkien, J. R. R. "On Fairy Stories." In *Essays Presented to Charles Williams*, edited by C. S. Lewis, 38–89. Grand Rapids: Eerdmans, 1977.

www.ingramcontent.com/pod-product-compliance
Lightning Source LLC
Chambersburg PA
CBHW030857170426
43193CB00009BA/645